ESSENTIALS OF
SPIRITUAL
WARFARE

EQUIPPED
TO WIN
THE BATTLE

A. SCOTT MOREAU

Harold Shaw Publishers
Wheaton, Illinois

ISBN 0-87788-167-7

Edited by Robert Bittner and Mary Horner Collins
Cover design by David LaPlaca

Library of Congress Cataloging-in-Publication Data

Moreau, A. Scott, 1955-
    Essentials of spiritual warfare : equipped to win the battle / A. Scott
    Moreau.
       p. cm.
    Includes bibliographical references.
    ISBN 0-87788-167-7
    1. Spiritual warfare. I. Title.
    BV4509.5.M664 1997
    235'.4—dc21   97-9817
                                                CIP

03   02   01   00   99   98

10 9 8 7 6 5 4 3 2

What reviewers say about *Essentials of Spiritual Warfare:*

"I highly recommend this book on spiritual warfare by Dr. Moreau. It is biblically based, personally relevant, and culturally sensitive. We simply cannot ignore the reality of the spiritual world, and this book offers a balanced understanding of the spiritual battle we are in." —*Neil T. Anderson (Ed.D., D.Min.), founder and president of Freedom in Christ Ministries*

"This is the best introduction to spiritual warfare on the market. Scott Moreau lays an excellent biblical foundation before dealing with the more difficult issues. His book is very readable and one that I will recommend to people in my church and students I teach.—*Clinton E. Arnold (Ph.D.), professor of New Testament, Talbot School of Theology*

"Dr. Moreau lays a solid foundation for dealing with the current debate on spiritual warfare. Avoiding a fascination with the sensational, he reminds us that the battle lies at the heart of our calling as Christians to righteousness and life.—*Paul G. Hiebert (Ph.D.), professor of Anthropology and Missions, Trinity International University*

"Scott Moreau's background as a professor and missionary are woven together in this biblical and practical book. His dealing with territorial spirits gives an excellent and balanced perspective. This book is a must for those seeking help with personal spiritual battles or those desiring to help others toward spiritual victory."—*N. James Logan (D.D.), pastoral counselor, International Center for Biblical Counseling*

ESSENTIALS OF SPIRITUAL WARFARE

Contents

Acknowledgments

Special thanks are always in order in the production of any book. Mine go to two communities in particular. The first group is my students. Leanne Winters and Larry Fuhrer offered invaluable input that resulted in several changes. The students who took my Spiritual Conflict course at Wheaton Graduate School in the spring semester of 1997 also provided numerous challenges to my thinking and suggestions for improvement and thereby significantly strengthened the book. From that class, I especially need to thank John Watson and Jim Apker. John's paper on the results of spiritual warfare thinking in La Resistencia, Argentina, is summarized as an illustration in chapter 10. Jim's paper on binding Satan confirmed some of my own thinking and added to my discussion in chapter 12.

The other group of people I would like to thank is the editorial team at Harold Shaw who significantly smoothed out my rough work, helped me think more clearly, and kept the book from getting too dusty. The strengths of this work are a credit to these two communities who worked together with me. The weaknesses remain my responsibility!

I also wish to express my deep love for and appreciation of my wife and children, the proving ground of whether my writing matches my living. Finally, to my "invisible" audience, I would deeply appreciate any feedback you might have to offer. I can be reached through Harold Shaw Publishers, P. O. Box 567, Wheaton, IL 60189.

Introduction

When I was approached about writing a book on spiritual warfare, I was delighted to accept. I have taught on this subject for more than a decade, on the graduate level here in America and in Africa. So it was exciting to finally take some concentrated time and distill the teaching, thinking, writing, and ministry with which I have been involved. While many books have been written on the topic of spiritual warfare in the last fifteen years, I feel that none have given an overview combining *what* spiritual warfare involves, *why* we are engaged in it, and *how* we can fight the daily battles we face. All three of these areas are part of the essential knowledge we need to be fully equipped to stand firm against the enemy's attacks. Let me explain what I mean.

Focusing only on the hows of doing spiritual warfare, without understanding the reasons behind them, can lead to ritualistic or magical thinking. Ritualistic thinking says, "If I just walk through a certain process once, then I never need worry about spiritual warfare again." Magical thinking reasons, "Once I know the right prayer formula, I can stop Satan's attacks." Both of these approaches miss the *relational foundation* of our warfare—our relationship with God and with others, and our relationship to Satan—and relationships do not work by invoking ritual or through the use of magic. It's the truth of who God is and who we are in Christ that enables us to fight the enemy, not just a formula.

On the other hand, studying the whys of spiritual battle without the hows can lead to sterility in our Christian walk. The person who knows the why and does not apply it to his or her life falls into the same trap as the demons, who believe in God and yet shudder in fear (James 2:19). Our schools and churches are filled with people who have an awareness of what is right, but who are unable to put that into practice in daily life. I find this a struggle in my own life, and writing this book has forced me to examine my own life once again.

In addition, many spiritual warfare books on the market are either popular accounts with good stories but little "meat" or more purely academic treatments that do not touch the hearts and lives of readers. I have tried to blend both of these perspectives here and have consciously written with the average churchgoer or new Christian in mind. So, this book is not intended to be an academic treatise, though it would be of use in an introductory course on spiritual warfare. It is not intended to cover the whole of spiritual warfare exhaustively, though I have tried to be reasonably comprehensive. I hope it will be useful for personal enrichment, for small group study, and for courses dealing with spiritual warfare or spiritual growth.

It has been my goal to encourage you to consider the spiritual battles being waged for people the world over. My prayer is that you will be as enriched in reading it as I have been in writing it, and that it will equip you to meet the challenge of spiritual warfare from a position of deeper insight and richer faith. Ultimately, my hope is that it will lead you into a more intimate knowledge of our Creator as revealed through the pages of Scripture, which is the repository for all of the spiritual armor necessary to maintain the victory in the encounters we face.

1

Getting the Big Picture

I will never forget a hot, lazy afternoon in rural Ntonjeni, a small village in northern Swaziland, where I taught general science in a public high school. During class a student suddenly slumped to the floor and began writhing and groaning. I thought she was experiencing an epileptic seizure. But the next day, and for the rest of the school year, she seemed fine. I assumed the event was over.

I later found out, however, that my Swazi students had a completely different explanation: what had happened was a result of love magic. They knew that a young man had an unreturned love for my student. Being rebuffed in his efforts, he had resorted to a traditional sorcerer, who called up spirits to torment the girl until she gave in to her suitor's wishes. I asked a Christian student how she interpreted what had happened. She said that the love magic explanation was the right one and that she had also been a victim of this magic before she came to Christ. Christians, she told me, were immune to it.

The same event, but two different lenses through which to view it. On one side, my Western background predisposed me to look for a physical reason for the seizure. I was the American science teacher struggling to get my students to believe atoms existed even though they could not see them. On the other side, my students, from their African perspective, looked for a spiritual reason for the seizure. They struggled with my failure to recognize that spirits existed in daily life. Didn't I realize that, like the wind, invisible spirits still can be seen by their effects?

Is one side completely right, and the other completely wrong? Is there a way to integrate and balance these two ways of viewing reality? One Old Testament incident may help illustrate the dilemma we often face in explaining spiritual realities.

King David, against God's will, decided to take a census to determine the size of his army. The issue was one of faith: Was David willing to trust God to provide for him, or was he trusting in his own earthly resources? In a moment of weakness, he made his choice. Two passages tell the story, yet each gives a remarkably different picture: "Satan rose up against Israel and incited David to take a census of Israel" (1 Chron. 21:1) and "Again the anger of the Lord burned against Israel, and he incited David against them, saying, 'Go and take a census of Israel and Judah'" (2 Sam. 24:1).

The author of 1 Chronicles focuses on Satan's role as the one who actually was used by God to incite David. The author of 2 Samuel focuses on God's role in provoking David because of his wrath against Israel. The variety of perspectives on the same event is at the center of the debates about understanding evil spirits and our approach to spiritual warfare in the contemporary world. The two biblical accounts do not contradict each other; they are complementary views of the same event. Each has a different focus and purpose in the perspective presented. Both are true.

Balance or Tension?

Many Christians writing on spiritual warfare propose that we need a *balanced* perspective on the issue. They say that we must balance our thinking between Satan's actions and our own sin. However, one problem I have with this approach is that most people, no matter what their perspective, believe their position is the only balanced one. Because of this tendency, I prefer to think of holding the extremes in tension rather than in balance.

The Bible clearly teaches that demons are both real and a real source of problems. We are warned to be alert because Satan prowls like a roaring lion. We are told to put on spiritual armor so that we can stand against attacks from spirits. We know or read of people who have fallen from the church because of demonic influence. Yet, at the same time, we are also told that we are responsible for our choices and actions before God. We cannot blame the devil; we must acknowledge our own culpability. We are called children of the King, reminded that the enemy cannot touch us, and told that the One in us is greater than the one in the world. The Bible does not teach that all sicknesses or mental problems are the results of demonic attacks; yet, we are told that some problems do result from demonic work and that demons are routed through direct encounters. While we can rest in God's provision, we also read that Paul prayed three times for God to remove a "thorn in the flesh" brought about by an angel of Satan, and God did not remove it. Ultimate victory is guaranteed, but our personal struggles do not always paint that picture very clearly.

All of these facts must be held in tension and not simply explained away so that our theological system looks good and tidy. I believe maintaining this tension best equips us to meet the challenge of spiritual warfare today.

Getting Equipped

The first step of getting ready for spiritual warfare is recognizing that spiritual warfare is fought in four ways: by engaging the truth, putting off sin, putting on righteousness, and exercising our authority in Christ to resist the enemy's attacks. We constantly move from one of these arenas to another depending on our life's circumstances. As figure 1 illustrates, engaging truth—

knowing and applying it—undergirds our work in all of the other areas. It is the foundation on which we stand, the battlefield on which we fight, and a weapon that we use in the battle.

We must engage the truth.

The central importance of knowing, believing, claiming, and living out the truth revealed in the Bible cannot be overstated. Simply knowing what is right is not enough; our knowledge must be exercised faithfully. This is what I mean by *engaging* truth.

In Genesis 3 we see that truth was distorted by the serpent, and this distortion was the means of the deception and fall of

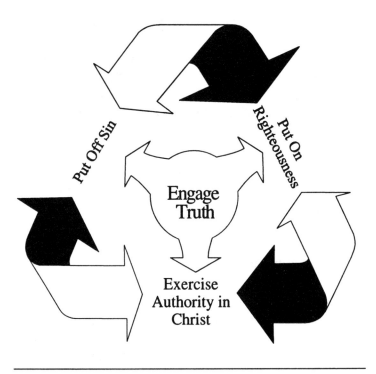

Figure 1
Engaging Truth: The Foundation of Spiritual Warfare

Adam and Eve. Jesus tells the Jews in John 8 that through knowing and obeying his teaching they will know truth and that this truth will set them free. He prays in John 17 that God would sanctify us by truth. The apostle Paul writes to the Romans that people are condemned because they exchanged God's truth for lies. To the Corinthians he writes that love rejoices in the truth rather than delighting in evil. In Paul's letter to the Galatians he chastises Peter for not living according to the truth. The first weapon of spiritual armor that he mentions to the Ephesians is the belt of truth. The Philippians are told to keep their minds reflecting on truth; the Thessalonians, that people are perishing because they refuse to love the truth. Timothy is reminded that God desires all people to be saved and come to knowledge of the truth. James tells us to bring back any who wander from the truth, and Peter writes that we are purified by obeying the truth. It's clear that the truth of the gospel undergirds every part of our faith.

There are many elements of this truth that apply specifically to spiritual warfare, but none are more central than understanding who God is, who we are as God's people, and who Satan is. If we fail to understand these three areas, we risk rushing headlong into battle not only unprepared but also set up for disaster. In the first section of this book we will look at facets of Christian truth that are of particular importance in meeting the challenge of spiritual warfare.

We must practice spiritual disciplines.

The second and third ways of fighting spiritual warfare include the battle with sin and the practice of living in godly ways. They are two sides of the same coin, inextricably linked together. On one side is the fact of sin and the necessity of putting off evil practices and attitudes. On the other side is replacing those actions and attitudes with godly habits. These practices reflect what is often called the Christian disciplines. They include, but are not limited to, loving God and people through confessing sin and repentance, forgiving each other, prayer, Bible study, Scripture memorization, and worship. The spiritual disciplines will be discussed in greater detail in the second section of this book.

We must exercise our authority.

Over the course of some months, Marge called me several times asking for a prayer that she could say to bless her home. (All names and circumstances have been changed throughout this book to ensure privacy.) Marge felt her home was cursed. She is not alone in wanting to resist Satan by finding the "right prayers" or going to the right person who has experience and power in this area. All of us tend to expect quick fixes to problems that took years to develop. I receive many calls from people like Marge, people wanting to bless a house or silence the evil voices they hear. They really do want to resist Satan, but they want to do it with an "instant" version of spiritual warfare.

According to the Bible, resisting Satan involves our "defense"— the protective "armor" Paul tells us to put on in Ephesians 6: truth, righteousness, the gospel of peace, hope in salvation, faith, and the Word of God. Acquire these disciplines, Paul says, and you will be prepared for the battle. It also involves an "offense"—exercising the authority we have been given in Christ and confronting spirits who would rob us of the full, meaningful life God has promised.

The Fronts of Spiritual Warfare

There are at least five different fronts on which spiritual battle is waged, and no exploration of spiritual warfare can be complete without considering these. I can only introduce each area here, but further discussion of the implications for spiritual warfare on these levels is done throughout the book. These five areas are not discrete and isolated from each other. Rather, they may be thought of as a set of overlapping circles that at any time can include individuals, groups, congregations, cultures, and the cosmos.

1. *The personal front.* This is our participation in the internal spiritual battles of daily life, and is the foundation for all of the other fronts. This front involves our minds: what we think about God, Satan, ourselves, and others and how we discipline our thoughts.

2. *The interpersonal or "each other" front.* This refers to our efforts to help others who are under attack and involves the ways we can challenge and encourage them. Warfare on this front can include anything from one-on-one counseling to small group ministry.

3. *The local church front.* This battlefront is spiritual warfare that may happen within local churches. It might be centered in an individual or a small group of people, but its impact affects the whole church.

4. *The systemic front.* This is the struggle against the domination systems that make up our societies—the cultural, political, economic, and even religious systems. In effect they are the manifestations of what 1 John 2:15-17 calls the "world"—all things that oppose God and his kingdom order. Warfare at this level involves our fight against the ungodly ways our culture controls and shapes our lives.

5. *The cosmic front.* This is the unseen front of warfare in which angels and demons engage each other in conflict under God's sovereign control. This area is one that remains out of human sight. We see only a few brief glimpses in Scripture (Daniel 10:4–11:1), and nowhere are we told that this is a front of direct human involvement.

Take Time to Reflect

The first section of this book lays out what we need to know about who God is, who Satan is, and who we are as human beings. Sprinkled throughout this section are reflection questions for you to consider, to help you engage the truths you are reading about. It's easy to read quickly for head knowledge, but I encourage you to take time to think through the issues as they apply to your life.

This may require regular breaks from the book to allow the Holy Spirit access to your heart. As you read, ask God to give you insights into his Word. Let him convict you of things you need to confess. Let him challenge you to step out in faith, trusting him in all areas of life. Let him write with the pen of his Holy Spirit on your heart the mighty truths of his love for you. Trust him to lead you to respond as he wants you to.

My prayer is that you will use this book as a tool for growth as well as a weapon for spiritual battle and that, in your reading, praying, meditating, and applying, you will find yourself being transformed into the image of your loving Creator.

I.
Engaging the Truth

2

God Is Still in Charge

After a decade of missionary work in Africa, my wife and I returned to the United States to work and live. Shortly after settling in, we were bombarded with the range of feelings that hits anyone readjusting to his or her own culture after a long absence. I had a one-year contract to teach, but after that things were hazy. We had been generously offered a furnished home at a very low rent, but we could live there only one year. We felt we had a year to breathe and get our feet on the ground, but we didn't know what was coming after that.

This was my first time out of the shelter of a mission agency and the financial support of generous donors. Relying on the goodwill contributions of others for our salary had brought with it a sense of comfort and protection: as long as we had supporters, we had job security. Without that support, I personally felt a heavy responsibility.

In the middle of all our adjustments, I began noticing the lottery. I saw the winning numbers on television, read them in the newspaper, and heard them on the radio. I saw the prize amounts on billboards and the exuberant winners in ads. I heard the jingles over and over on the radio. They seemed to take up permanent residence in my brain. People who had lived in the United States during the 1980s and early 1990s had adjusted to this, but it hit me all at once. Combine this with the fact that I was feeling insecure in my ability to meet my financial responsibilities, and it is no wonder that I began to meditate on the lottery and the idea of instant wealth. *Just think,* I reasoned to myself, *my tithe would be more than my present salary! I wouldn't have to worry about a job anymore.*

As one who had served in Christian ministry and was now preparing others to do the same, I instinctively knew that actually buying a lottery ticket would cross a line that was wrong for me. But that didn't stop me from daydreaming about it. When I walked to school each morning, I rationalized that God could let someone else buy the winning ticket and then lose it in a place where I could find it! Over the next few months I developed the habit of what I now call "lottery lust." Though I didn't buy a ticket, I thought about it, hoped for it, and believed it would provide the security blanket I so desperately wanted.

This went on for several months before God finally got my attention. One cold, snowy day in January, as I was driving, I listened to a tape from a spiritual warfare conference. The speaker said, "Do you know what's wrong with the lottery? It is calling us to live our lives on the horizontal level. It is built on the assumption that money meets our real needs. It is built on a lie." His statements hit me like a bombshell. I had been focusing on the horizontal; I had been thinking that money (and financial security) would meet my needs. I had forgotten that God had faithfully met my physical needs every step of the way. I had lost sight of the *truth.*

Holding on to the Truth

Of course, thinking about the lottery was not the issue—*believing* that winning the lottery would meet my needs was the issue. I wanted security, but I had lost track of the simple truth that God has promised to provide for his children. His track record of faithfulness in the life of my family was flawless. Somehow I had allowed myself to think that having a guaranteed income for the rest of my life would make me happy, meet my deepest needs, and provide all the security I needed. I had fallen for a lie.

Each of us faces a moment-by-moment battle for our minds, the battle to know and believe truth. I call this the personal front of spiritual warfare. It is the approach Satan took when he tempted Adam and Eve to take the forbidden fruit. God had told them one thing; Satan had to convince them that God's way was wrong. He had to loosen their hold on what was truth. And so the battle that began in Eden continues even today, in little ways, in the heart and mind of every believer.

To be fit and equipped for personal spiritual warfare I must know, believe, and apply biblical truths about spiritual warfare. I must know who God is, who I am, and who Satan is. *Knowing* truth is not the final goal; *believing and acting on* that truth is. I must let my commitment to truth be seen in the way I live my life. That is, at any time during my "lottery lust," I would have passed a doctrinal test on God's sovereignty and his willingness to meet my needs with flying colors. The problem was not that I didn't know about him or his intentions. It was that I did not apply what I knew to the needs I felt. Truth was in my head, but I had not let it filter down into my actions.

Our challenge is to get the truth into our minds and allow it to infect us so that we are renewed in all that we think and do. As you read through this section, ask yourself what this means to you today at work, at home, with your family, with your friends. The reflection questions provided after each section may help to stimulate your thinking. Ask God to so infect you with truth that you become a contagious carrier of it!

What Is Your God Like?

What images come to mind when you hear that God is the sovereign Creator of the universe? That God has no equal and is keenly interested in working out his designs for the universe?

That God is completely just, completely loving, completely merciful? That God cares not just for the created order but for you personally? That he is interested not only in the big events of life but also in the daily grind?

Do these truths leave you cold, excite you, or frighten you? Is your God a Big Brother watching your every step, just waiting for you to step out of line so he can clobber you? Or is he a distant Being who made the universe and now is just sitting back and watching life unfold?

What does the Bible tell us about God? Of course, to answer that question fully would take up more space than this book will allow. There are several ideas and passages in appendix A to help you begin answering that question. In this chapter, let's focus on several points of God's nature and character that can be gleaned from the account of the Creation and Fall found in Genesis 1–3.

My concern throughout this chapter is your heartfelt response to the truth. Most Christians agree that God is in charge, but they forget that powerful truth when things go wrong in their lives. And even many of those who say that God is loving still have difficulty connecting with that idea in a meaningful way. Who, then, is God? More important, who is *your* God? Whether you've been a Christian for a few months or many years, as you read the following, ask yourself what you really think about God and what difference that makes in your struggles with the enemy.

God Is Our Father

God is our heavenly Father, but that picture should not be confused with what many of us have seen in our human fathers. Stephen, whose father was cold, distant, and demanding, never really felt accepted by God. Craig, whose father had abandoned the family, felt that God would not be there when times got tough. Denise, whose dad had been involved in an adulterous affair for over a decade while serving as a church leader, saw God as a hypocrite who said one thing and did another. Debbie's dad had physically abused her, and she viewed God as a violator of people. Sharon is a young woman whose most vivid memory of childhood was seeing a friend burn to death. She had a terribly difficult time imagining that God really cared for her.

All of these people experienced deeply significant events in their childhood. Those experiences formed lasting impressions that were transferred to God. For Stephen, God could never be satisfied. For Craig, God was the one who was never there. For Denise, God didn't keep his promises. For Debbie, God was abusive, and she had little desire to connect with him. For Sharon, God did not answer prayer.

When God is called "Father" in the Bible, it does not refer to gender, for God is neither male nor female. Rather, the fact that God is "Father" indicates both his role as our Creator and the type of relationship he desires to have with his creation: "So God created man in his own image, . . . male and female he created them" (Gen. 1:27).

Engaging the Truth
➤ *When you think of God as a Father, what images come to mind?*
➤ *In what ways are you tempted to transfer your feelings about your biological father onto God? How might the enemy use those feelings to block your relationship with God and your desire for intimacy with him?*

God Is the Sovereign Creator

The first two chapters of Genesis paint a marvelous picture of who God is. We see creativity at its height, with God making everything that exists. Despite the controversies over the mechanics of creation, no one who takes the Bible seriously debates the fact that God is the One who did the work.

In modern terms, God is the inventor of creation. He owns the patent, and he deserves the royalties. You and I give him the royalties he deserves when we live our lives the way he designed them to be lived. This is what it means to glorify, or acknowledge and honor, God as the Creator.

The first test of God's sovereignty was in the command he gave to Adam in Genesis 2:16-17: "You are free to eat from any tree in the garden; but you must not eat from the tree of the knowledge of good and evil, for when you eat of it you will surely die." God's nature is to be generous, and his design for Adam and Eve was that they would have free access to every type of food. There was one exception: they were not to eat food they were not yet ready to eat. God was not being mean in the prohibition. He was simply giving Adam and Eve the chance to choose how they would live. The command was clear—as were the consequences. There were no hidden tricks or traps, only the exercise of the Creator's sovereignty.

After Adam and Eve chose disobedience and death, and sin entered creation, God's sovereignty was still intact. God judged the serpent, who could not stand (either literally or metaphorically) before him. God expelled Adam and Eve from the Garden and prevented their reentry. By these actions, God demonstrated that those who are the crown of his created order, as well as the tempter who would draw them away from righteousness, are still subject to him.

Engaging the Truth
➤ *How do you picture God's sovereignty working in your daily life? (Do you see God waiting to pounce on your mistakes or controlling events in ways that anger, frustrate, or intimidate you?)*
➤ *In what ways might your understanding of God's control be skewed? How does that affect the way you relate to him?*

God Is the Faithful Lover and Provider

As the Creator, God naturally loves what he created. One sign of that love is his *physical* provision for human beings. The freedom to eat that he gave to Adam and Eve applied to every tree, with one exception. God's generosity is unlimited within the realm of obedience to his created order. He provided more than Adam and Eve could ever need, and he gave them unrestricted access to the things that would be good for them. The only thing he prohibited was the thing for which they were not ready and which would ultimately harm them.

We also see God as a faithful lover in the creation of Eve. Adam was unique in the created order, and there was not a suitable partner for him. God supplied Adam's need through Eve, and Adam's joyous shout of praise on seeing Eve (Gen. 2:23-24) tells us how God feels about meeting our needs. He created us as people who have the capacity to love, and he created other people to meet our need to love.

Before God made Adam and Eve, he made everything else that they would need. The abundance of the whole earth was provided for them before they were even created. Their original task was not so much to provide for themselves as to take advantage of the provision God had already supplied. Even after the Fall, God remained a gracious provider. In addition to the promise of the eventual destruction of the serpent, God accommodated himself to the fact that the man and woman were now ashamed of their nakedness, and he provided skins for them to wear (Gen. 3:21).

Another picture of God as faithful is seen in his *spiritual* provision for these first rebels in the Garden. They disobeyed and God confronted them. They tried to hide and God found them. They blamed him and God promised relief. They chose death and God promised new life. The fall into sin did not stop

God from being faithful to those he created. And the One who met Adam and Eve's deepest human needs can still meet our needs today.

Engaging the Truth
➤ *What difference does it make to know that God really loves you?*
➤ *What circumstances in your life tempt you to worry and fret that God won't provide for you? How can you trust him more?*

God Is the Persistent Initiator

After Adam and Eve sinned, God did not wait for them to come to him. He sought them out. "Then the man and his wife heard the sound of the Lord God as he was walking in the garden in the cool of the day, and they hid from the Lord God among the trees of the garden. But the Lord God called to the man, 'Where are you?'" (Gen. 2:8-9).

Even though they hid, God called out to them—and not because he did not know where they were. He wanted them to understand that he cared enough to meet them on their own terms. When they responded, he exposed what they had done. He was not being vindictive. Rather, bringing their sin to light was an act of mercy and love. Once Adam and Eve admitted their sin, God hinted at a day when the woman's progeny would "crush the serpent's head" (Gen. 3:15), a reference to the coming of God's Son, Jesus. This was another sign that God would persist in his redeeming love for humanity.

God is also a *righteous judge*. As the sovereign, holy Creator, God must judge the actions of those who have violated his created order. Adam and Eve were no exception. They had proven themselves unable to withstand the temptation to disobedience and had to endure the consequences. God judged the serpent, promising Satan's eventual destruction (Gen. 3:14-15).

He judged the woman and the man (3:16-19) in ways designed to remind them of what they had lost and, therefore, drive them back to his love and protection. God does not take sin lightly. But his judgments are never separate from his love.

Engaging the Truth
➤ *What signs in your life do you see of God's persistent love?*
➤ *Is it hard for you to picture God as a judge? Why or why not?*

The Foundation

So in conclusion, *who is God to you?* Ask God to give you the vision to see him as he is, not as you have made him out to be. God's desire is that we connect with him as a close, personal, awesome One who graciously chose and delivered us simply because he loves us. If you have a hard time connecting with God, or if your view of him is more frightening than comforting, find some trusted Christian friends with whom you can talk. Study together about who God is and how images from your own background and development have affected the way you are inclined to see him. Satan does not care which distortion of God you and I accept. He is only concerned that we accept *some* counterfeit in place of the truth. Without this foundation of seeing God as he really is, it will be difficult to be fully equipped for the challenge of personal spiritual warfare. Let's turn now to Jesus, God the Son, who has secured our victory.

3

Jesus Won the War

At the turn of the century during British colonial rule in India, a government administrator was traveling in the jungle south of Calcutta. While approaching a small government house they were to stay in, a servant bolted out of the house, white as a sheet. He had found a twenty-foot-long python curled around a piece of furniture. A full-grown python is deadly and powerful and can swallow a deer or a pig whole. The men locked the python inside and checked their ammunition. They had one bullet that was strong enough to kill a snake of this size, and only if it was a direct hit to the head. Taking careful aim, the administrator shot the python right in the head. But rather than dying, the python became crazed, thrashing about violently, smashing furniture, knocking out lights, and demolishing the interior of the small house. Finally, after an hour and a half of this, the snake died.

What a vivid picture of the spiritual battle we face. God dealt Satan a crushing blow through Jesus' death on the cross. We could say that we are now living in that "one and a half hours," as it were, and Satan is thrashing about in evil destruction. But the fatal blow has been struck. On the cross, the Son of God won the ultimate battle over evil and death! Jesus had a keen understanding of the reality of spiritual conflict. Let's look at two fascinating portraits of Jesus in the New Testament that help us see his view of spiritual warfare and how he fought the enemy's onslaughts.

Learning from the Master

In the first story, Jesus is emaciated and weary from forty days
of fasting. He stumbles across a wilderness landscape that is
unearthly in its desolation, especially in the heat of the noonday
sun. At his moment of weakness, just when the pains of hunger
after weeks without food are at their peak, the enemy comes—
absent when Jesus was at his strongest, suddenly present when
Jesus is weakest. This is the context of Satan's temptation of
Jesus as told in Matthew's Gospel:

> Then Jesus was led by the Spirit into the desert to be tempted
> by the devil. After fasting forty days and forty nights, he was
> hungry. The tempter came to him and said, "If you are the Son
> of God, tell these stones to become bread."
>
> Jesus answered, "It is written: 'Man does not live on bread
> alone, but on every word that comes from the mouth of God.'"
>
> Then the devil took him to the holy city and had him stand on
> the highest point of the temple. "If you are the Son of God," he
> said, "throw yourself down. For it is written: 'He will command
> his angels concerning you, and they will lift you up in their hands,
> so that you will not strike your foot against a stone.'"
>
> Jesus answered him, "It is also written: 'Do not put the Lord
> your God to the test.'"
>
> Again, the devil took him to a very high mountain and
> showed him all the kingdoms of the world and their splendor.
> "All this I will give you," he said, "if you will bow down and
> worship me."
>
> Jesus said to him, "Away from me, Satan! For it is written:
> 'Worship the Lord your God, and serve him only.'"
>
> Then the devil left him, and angels came and attended him.
> (Matt. 4:1-11)

In the second story a short while later, we see an entirely different picture. Imagine you are a disciple of Jesus. You have just sailed across the Sea of Galilee, and it is late in the afternoon. You are tying up the boat so it won't drift. You hear a scream and turn around. A wild-looking man is tearing down the path straight to Jesus. He falls on his knees before your Master, screaming at the top of his lungs—defiance and humility commingled. What could be happening?

Running to Jesus' aid, you notice the man's nakedness and the scars where he has been shackled and where he has cut himself. Then you realize that he came out from a nearby field of tombs. No sane person would live naked among the tombs. Suddenly it dawns on you—this man is controlled by a demon! You hear Jesus commanding the demon to come out of the man. Nothing seems to happen. Jesus asks his name, and you know he is talking to the demon. The answer is, "Legion, for we are many." Six thousand demons? Then something amazing happens: The demons beg Jesus for clemency. Their spokesman even asks Jesus to swear by God's name, as if the demon's rebellion against God really doesn't matter when it comes to God's name. The tormentor is asking not to be tormented!

Jesus grants the demons permission to enter a herd of pigs nearby. Being an Orthodox Jew, you have never touched pig meat, and you can't imagine anyone who would. *What a fitting end,* you think, *unclean spirits going into unclean animals.* Suddenly the pigs go crazy, rushing down a cliff and drowning in the water below. When you turn back to the man, he is sitting up, restored and sane. He even asks if he can join your group, but Jesus tells him to return to his home and tell everyone what has happened to him.

Meanwhile, the pig herders come down demanding an explanation. They see the man, and a look of recognition comes into their eyes. Expressing consternation at his sanity at their expense, their hearts harden. They urge Jesus to go away, apparently caring more about their livestock than for the soul of an afflicted man (see Mark 5:2-20).

We learn many things about Jesus and about engaging in spiritual warfare from these two events. As in the prior chapter, I invite you to consider the reflection questions following each section to allow these observations to sift down into your own life.

Jesus Trusted God and Chose Obedience

At the start of the temptation, Jesus was hungry. The temptation here was to meet a necessary goal (physical sustenance) in a way that showed lack of faith that God would provide. In saying no to Satan, *Jesus trusted that God would supply his needs.* At the end, after Satan was gone, Matthew says that angels came and ministered to Jesus. The word used for *ministered* literally means "table service." God met Jesus' need for food. It is critical for us to see that Jesus did not take the first solution offered for his hunger. Instead, he waited for God's answer.

Each time the tempter made an offer, Jesus responded with Scripture. *He trusted God's Word to be true and powerful.* Pocket Bibles did not exist in Jesus' day; he had studied and memorized the Old Testament Scriptures. He was prepared for anything Satan would offer—not simply because he had verses memorized, but because he knew the meaning of the Scriptures hidden in his heart. This is proof-texting at its best: applying appropriately the truths of God's Word in light of present circumstances. It was good enough for Jesus, and it is good enough for us.

In the second temptation, when Jesus was challenged to jump off the temple, Satan taunts him: "Do you *really* trust God? Then prove it, and prove his love for you. Just trust him to protect you when you jump." Resisting and walking faithfully through this temptation gave Jesus the strength to face the depths of agony he would experience later in the Garden of Gethsemane, when he resolved to go forward and die on the cross for us. Jesus' goal was victory over the enemy through *trust in and complete obedience to God's way.* Our goal is to be the same. Though he could have called literally thousands of angels to his aid, just as Satan suggested, Jesus chose instead to walk the kingdom path.

Engaging the Truth
➤ *What are some of the benefits of memorizing portions of the Bible for spiritual growth?*
➤ *What do you think enabled Jesus to choose obedience to God rather than Satan's plan?*

Jesus Came to Engage in War

The book of 1 John informs us that Jesus came to destroy Satan's works (1 John 3:8). This does not refer to Satan's works in some distant, general sense; it includes those works as found in *our* lives. Knowing that all humanity had been dominated by the enemy, just as the possessed man was, Jesus came to destroy that domination and set us free.

The religious leaders of Jesus' day, jealous of his authority and popularity, accused him of casting out the demons by the power of "Beelzebub," one of the names for the prince of demons (Luke 11:14-20). Jesus replied that it would be absurd for Satan to empower Jesus to work against Satan. Jesus went on to tell a parable: "When a strong man, fully armed, guards his own house, his possessions are safe. But when someone stronger attacks and overpowers him, he takes away the armor in which the man trusted and divides up the spoils" (Luke 11:21-22). Here, Jesus is the stronger man, and Satan is the one whom Jesus binds. (I discuss the issue of binding Satan in more detail in chapter 12.) You and I are the valuables being plundered from Satan's house. When a person comes to Christ for salvation, he or she has been plundered from Satan's domain and set free to obey God. We know that Jesus is stronger than Satan—he wins every encounter with demons! Jesus is the victor in this war.

Though engaged in warfare, Jesus always demonstrated a real *compassion for the people who were victims of evil spirits.* The Gerasene demoniac's own community treated him like an animal, trying to chain him down from time to time. He had always broken the chains and returned to the tombs where he lived. On the human level, perhaps he was showing how he felt about himself, that he was already as good as dead. On the spiritual level, the demons were publicly demonstrating their control and showing that no mere human could force them to let go.

Then Jesus entered the picture. He treated this man as a human being created in God's image. Empowered by God's Spirit, he commanded the demons to set the man free. As a result, this once insane and naked man was left clothed and in his right mind. But Jesus didn't leave it at that. Having set the man free, Jesus gave him a task: go home and tell his story. With this, Jesus lovingly helped restore public dignity to the man. Imagine what this meant to such an outcast.

Engaging the Truth
➤ *Why do you think the religious leaders accused Jesus of being in league with Satan?*
➤ *What dangers are there in seeking to minister to victims of demonic attack without remembering that they are made in the image of God?*

Jesus Exercised Authority

Jesus showed his absolute authority when the demons responded to his verbal eviction orders without question. Jesus did not even have to be present for them to obey (see Matt. 15:22-28 and Mark 7:24-30). This does not mean, though, that there were no confrontations. Unlike the exorcists of that time, who used elaborate rituals and severe torture to cast out demons, Jesus simply spoke.

Those who saw this were astounded at his authority.

Notice that Jesus' path to victory came by *following God's rules of engagement rather than Satan's.* When the demons left the man and destroyed the pigs, they clearly revealed their ultimate destructive intentions for the man. In that day the sea was thought of as a gateway to the underworld. The fact that the pigs drowned in the sea would have had significance for the disciples, who might have seen it as a sign that Jesus had sent them to their destruction. In this dramatic object lesson, Jesus used the demons' desire for destruction as the means for bringing about judgment on the demons themselves. He showed that it is necessary, not to fight Satan on Satan's terms, but to oppose him using God's perspective.

Engaging the Truth
➤ *How does Jesus' authority over evil encourage your faith right now?*
➤ *Take some time to think and pray about creative ways to overcome evil with good.*

Jesus Understands Temptation

While all humans have been tempted, not one of us has reached the stage Jesus did. Tempted in every way, he never gave in. (Tempted in *any* way, I all too often give in!) Jesus knew how to obey God no matter the cost. He can relate to our struggles with sin, but his empathy goes even further. He knows what goes on in our minds as well as what we experience in life; nothing takes him by surprise. If we think of disappointment as being surprised by failure, you and I can never disappoint Jesus. What an encouragement to know that Jesus lived as a human being and understands our struggle from the inside!

The temptation in the wilderness was not Satan's last gamble; it was only his first attempt. In Luke's account of the temptation we are told that Satan left Jesus "until an opportune time" (Luke 4:13). Such future encounters came. When Peter rebuked Jesus for saying he would have to die on the cross, Jesus recognized Satan's voice in the words of his own disciple. When the crowds wanted to crown him king, he knew that political triumph was not the path God had prepared. And just before his death, Jesus was betrayed by Judas, one of his own, and then abandoned by the rest of the disciples.

Through each temptation experience, Jesus kept his focus on God's call. When Christ calls us to obedience in spite of opposition, he understands the agony, frustration, and fear we face. He knows how to walk us through the valley of death, giving us peace in knowing that he is with us, no matter what happens.

Engaging the Truth
➤ *What things do you appreciate about Jesus' example of facing temptations?*
➤ *What difference does it make to you to know that Jesus understands from the inside what temptation is really like?*

The Battle's Won

Like the fatally wounded python in our opening story, Satan is done for. The best and final example of God's ability to take the best plans of Satan and turn them upside down is the Cross, where Jesus became a curse and died for our sake (Gal. 3:10-15; Col. 2:15-19). At his crucifixion, rather than pursuing Satan's violent destruction, Jesus submitted himself to Satan's violence. He then demonstrated his power over Satan when he rose from the dead. Through Jesus' resurrection, death lost its grip on humanity. If we want to take part in Jesus' victory, we must walk in obedience to God rather than just reacting to Satan. We can rest in the fact that the Prince of eternity has already defeated the prince of this world.

4

Equipped by the Spirit

Jesus' temptation in the wilderness was not just some misguided adventure that he undertook on a whim. He was purposefully led by the Holy Spirit into the desert to be tested. *Whose side is the Spirit on?* you may wonder. It's clear that being filled with the Spirit, essential for Christians, does not stop Satan's attacks. We can also be assured that the Holy Spirit is for us and will provide a way through the wilderness. J. B. Phillips observed, "Every time we say, 'I believe in the Holy Spirit,' we mean that we believe that there is a living God able and willing to enter human personality and change it." Let's consider the role that the living God, through his Spirit, plays in empowering and supernaturally equipping us for victory. We can't do battle without him.

The Spirit Leads Us to Truth

The Gospel of John devotes five of twenty-one chapters to Jesus' teaching at the time of the Last Supper. Sprinkled throughout these five chapters are numerous references to the Holy Spirit, whom Jesus refers to as the *Spirit of truth:*

And I will ask the Father, and he will give you another Counselor to be with you for ever—the *Spirit of truth.* The world cannot accept him, because it neither sees him nor knows him. But you know him, for he lives with you and will be in you. (John 14:16-17, italics added)

When the Counselor comes, whom I will send to you from the Father, the *Spirit of truth* who goes out from the Father, he will testify about me. (15:26)

But when he, the *Spirit of truth,* comes, he will guide you into all truth. He will not speak on his own; he will speak only what he hears, and he will tell you what is yet to come. (16:13)

Ultimately, the Spirit has revealed the truth that we now have as the Bible. In our lives, he illuminates truth as we allow him to control and lead us. In light of Satan's fundamental desire to distort truth, then, it should not surprise us that there is more theological controversy and disagreement over the ministry of the Holy Spirit than any other member of the Trinity. Although we cannot here settle the controversies regarding the Holy Spirit, it is important to recognize how Satan wants to use theological differences to divide us. Since the Spirit has the task of leading us into truth, Satan will try to distort this leading any way he can. Satan is a liar. The Spirit's role as a revealer of truth is our foundation for spiritual warfare.

Engaging the Truth
> *In what ways have you seen Satan cause confusion about the Holy Spirit in your life or in your church?*
> *What does it mean to allow the Holy Spirit to control and lead us?*

The Spirit Exposes the World's Sin

A young man once went to hear the great seventeeth-century preacher George Whitefield in Plymouth, England. Whitefield recalls that the man said he came "to pick a hole in the preacher's coat; and the Holy Spirit picked a hole in his heart." The Spirit not only reveals truth but also exposes sin and convicts the world when it does not listen to truth.

> But I tell you the truth: It is for your good that I am going away. Unless I go away, the Counselor will not come to you; but if I go, I will send him to you. When he comes, he will convict the world of guilt in regard to sin and righteousness and judgment: in regard to sin, because men do not believe in me; in regard to righteousness, because I am going to the Father, where you can see me no longer; and in regard to judgment, because the prince of this world now stands condemned. (John 16:7-11)

The Spirit is like a "prosecutor" sent after Jesus' resurrection. One of his jobs is to convict the world, exposing and judging its values and its way of life and belief. Because the world has not believed in Jesus, the Spirit will expose and judge this fact. On a personal level, the Spirit brings feelings of guilt and shame on those who continue to rebel against God. He also uses these emotions in the lives of Christians to bring us to repentance. This is important in spiritual warfare. By repenting, we remove the burden of sin from our own hearts and minds, and Satan can no longer use that sin to accuse us or entangle us further in his schemes. We'll return to this theme of repentance later in chapter 9.

The Spirit will also expose the world to the fact that righteousness comes only from the work of Christ. We cannot earn it, which is good news. If we could earn it, then we would always be wondering if we have done enough. But righteousness comes as a gift, so we can rest in the fact that it has been earned on our behalf. Satan's attempts to make us believe that we can earn our way into heaven are thwarted when we trust the Spirit to teach us that righteousness comes only from Christ.

Finally, the Spirit will expose the fact of God's judgment on Satan, who already stands condemned before God. What a relief to know that Satan is condemned by God for his work in my life! I do not have to believe his accusations; I can rest in Christ's righteousness. When attacked, I can respond knowing that our destinies are settled in eternity—and that they are in opposite places. When Satan reminds me of sin that already has been confessed before Jesus and forgiven, by the power of the Spirit I can remind him that his standing before God has already been determined.

Engaging the Truth
➤ *What is the Holy Spirit's goal in exposing areas of sin in your life?*
➤ *How does knowing that the Holy Spirit is your ally in spiritual battle encourage you?*

The Spirit Points Us to Christ

Jesus tells the disciples that the Spirit's intention is to point us to Christ, not draw attention to himself. This is accomplished when the Spirit communicates Christ's directions to the church:

> [The Spirit] will bring glory to me by taking from what is mine and making it known to you. (John 6:14)

> But the Counselor, the Holy Spirit, whom the Father will send in my name, will teach you all things and will remind you of everything I have said to you. (John 14:26)

In spiritual warfare, the Spirit's job is to lead us in truth, enable us to apply truth in the midst of conflict, and, through it all, point us to the Christlike ways we are to respond.

In addition, the Spirit *unites in Christ.* According to 1 Corinthians 12:13, "we were all baptized by one Spirit into one body—whether Jews or Greeks, slave or free." Paul told the Ephesians that it was the Spirit who sealed us as members of Christ's body as a pledge from God of what is to come (Eph. 1:13-14). When Satan wants us to think that somehow we have not been good enough Christians or that there is something about us that God cannot redeem, the Spirit reminds us that we are God's children and belong to him (Rom. 8:16). Because of the Holy Spirit's work in our lives, you and I now belong to Christ.

Over a period of several months, a young man named Pete called me many times, wondering if he had lost his salvation over some small, picky misdemeanor he had committed. Typically, he would make minor vows before God and then break them. Instantly the mental accusations came: "You can't be a real Christian. Even if you *were,* now you've really done it. You don't dare hope for salvation." One of Pete's problems was that he listened to the clamor of the enemy's voice rather than the quiet confirmation of the Spirit in his heart.

Engaging the Truth
➤ *If the Spirit points us to Christ, how can you recognize when Satan is subtly steering you away from Christ? What can you do to get back on track?*
➤ *Have you ever doubted your salvation? What types of accusations were part of this temptation for you?*

The Spirit Equips the Church with Gifts

By all outward appearances, the church at Corinth seemed to have it all. With spiritual gifts in abundance and the personal instruction of the apostle Paul to guide them, they were empowered to take on the world. But things are not always what they seem.

The church in Corinth had a few problems. They had experienced God working in their midst, yet Paul addressed them as babes in Christ. They knew the freedom they had in Christ, but they were in danger of turning that freedom into licentious indulgence. They were taking each other to court, unable to decide issues within the church. Some were coming to the communion table drunk. In a city with a reputation for sexual promiscuity, some of the men were apparently visiting prostitutes. They were so casual about sexual relations that they were proud that one of their members was sleeping with his father's wife.

To this group Paul wrote the longest exposition on spiritual gifts in any of his New Testament letters. In 1 Corinthians 12–14 we see the Spirit's role in equipping the church with gifts as a means of preparing it for spiritual warfare. Though we cannot go into a detailed exposition of this entire section or a discussion of all the gifts, there are several lessons that can be drawn from this passage about the Spirit's work in relation to spiritual warfare.

The overriding general truth that stands out here is that the *Spirit has given the church what it needs to worship and serve God effectively.* While every Christian is gifted (Eph. 4:7), it is the Spirit who matches the gift(s) and the recipients as he wills. The diversity of gifts reflects the diversity of our needs as a body of believers. We need to know truth—and the gifts of wisdom, knowledge, prophecy, teaching, tongues and their interpretation lead us to that knowledge. We need to maintain vision and direction—and apostolic, pastoral, and administrative gifts help us to organize and accomplish our objectives. We need to grow—and evangelistic and prophetic gifts are provided to challenge the world to come to Christ.

In all of these areas, the Spirit enables us to fight the enemy's desire to break our communion with God and render us ineffective in his service. Here are a couple of ways that the gifts of the Holy Spirit help the church in battle.

The Spirit enables some believers to discern spirits.

Paul specifically mentions the gift of being able to discern spirits. Since Satan is able to counterfeit spiritual events, including prophecy, the working of miracles, and even demonic expulsion (Matt. 7:21-23), there are times when human intuition is simply not enough to know whether something is from God. This gift is tied to a supernatural awareness given by the Holy Spirit that enables the believers to distinguish demonic spirits from the Holy Spirit without having to see the fruit of the supernatural event or judge the doctrine of it. Great caution must be taken for those claiming this gift, since it can all too easily be turned to evil purposes in the form of witch-hunts.

The Spirit builds us into the body of Christ.

The Spirit's intention in giving gifts is not individual growth but growth as a body of Christians. The Spirit's gifts are community oriented; we have gifts not for our own sake but for the sake of the common good of Christ's body. They are gifts with a purpose beyond the enjoyment of the one who is gifted. By exercising the gifts appropriately, we grow together as a body. My gift is not primarily intended to help *me* grow, but for me to exercise so that *you* can grow. It is the Spirit's task to orchestrate the working together of gifts so that, as a community, we grow into what it means to be the "bride of Christ." This work is a preparation for heaven and what we will experience there, a foretaste that keeps us looking expectantly toward what eternity has in store.

Satan's hope is to twist the gifts of the Spirit for his purposes. Whether he gives us counterfeit gifts or persuades us to stop using our gifts or to use them for selfish and divisive purposes, his goal is the same: he desires to tear Christians apart. He wants us focused on ourselves rather than on Christ, or focused on gifts rather than the purposes for which those gifts were given.

Engaging the Truth
➤ *Have you ever had a hunch that things were not what they seemed? Could that be equated with the gift of discernment? Why or why not?*
➤ *What are the ways God has gifted you? How might these gifts be best employed in spiritual warfare?*

What Difference Does It Make?

We have spent a good deal of time in these chapters on basic truths about God, Jesus, and the Holy Spirit. The question now is not so much whether you know the truth, but how you are living in light of that truth. What difference does it make to you that God is the Creator? Does your life reflect the fact that he provides for your needs? What does it mean to you that Jesus did not overcome Satan by violence but by submission? Are you willing to submit your very life if obedience to God requires it? How does it affect you to know that the Holy Spirit wants to guide you into truth? Is it important to you that he has given you gifts not just for your self-esteem but for the benefit of those around you?

As we walk through other important issues in later chapters, you may want to come back to the truths here to remind yourself of who God is. Equipped with this solid foundation, you will be better prepared to understand who the enemy is and how he wants to steal, kill, and bring destruction to your life and the life of your church.

5

Facing the Enemy

Jennifer suffered abuse repeatedly as a child. In fact, her childhood was so traumatic that she remembers almost nothing of her life before the age of fourteen. She has two girlfriends who are trapped in an occult group in which they are being abused. Jennifer believes that "if Satan wants to get you, there is nothing you can do." She is convinced that once Satan has hold of a person, there is really no way out. From her tragic background and experience, in her heart and mind, she sees Satan as the one who exercises real power on earth.

Martha is just the opposite. She's a Christian, but she thinks that Satan does not really exist and that what people call spiritual warfare is nothing more than our own internal struggles. She believes that Satan is simply a symbol of the evil that lives in human hearts and that we need to stop trying to blame him for our own sinfulness. She admits that the Bible teaches about Satan and presents him as real. Still, she feels that only "primitive" cultures still believe in a literal devil and that the Bible reflects that way of thinking. To Martha, Satan is a remnant of old, irrelevant belief systems.

Tim takes a different approach. He believes that Satan is real, but he figures that as long as he leaves Satan alone, Satan will leave him alone. He is not too interested in spiritual warfare, afraid that he will stir up a hornet's nest of trouble by getting involved. He is also wary of the wild extremes, like seeing demons where none exist. He figures that God is all he needs to study and that knowing God will automatically protect him from Satan's attacks.

Will the Real Satan Stand Up?

I come across people like Jennifer, Martha, and Tim on a regular basis. They are representative of the variety of positions on Satan found in the Western church today. Jennifer is right that Satan wields huge influence today. Martha is correct in saying that we cannot blame Satan for all of our problems. Tim is right that we need to focus on God. However, all of them are wrong in that they either underemphasize or overemphasize our enemy. With such varied views, it is easy to see why it is important to explore carefully what the Bible says about Satan and the demons who follow him. The apostle Paul wrote in 2 Corinthians 2:11 that he was "not unaware of Satan's schemes." Following Paul's example, we will become more aware of Satan's schemes when we have a clearer picture of who he is.

Let's turn again to the two biblical stories of temptation we've been looking at for some revealing details about who Satan really is. In Genesis 3, Adam and Eve were tempted to disobey God. They took the serpent's advice, and all of us live in light of the tragic consequences. In the New Testament, three of the Gospels tell the story of Satan's temptation of Jesus. Unlike Adam and Eve, Jesus stood his ground and met the challenge the enemy presented. Today we enjoy the benefits of his success. Of course, these events do not show *all* that the Bible teaches about Satan. (For further study, see the section on the biblical teaching on Satan in appendix A.) But these stories offer important insights into the nature and character of the evil one who rebelled against his Creator—knowledge that is critical to have if we want to stand our ground in the challenges Satan brings.

Satan Is a Created Being

The Bible does not try to prove God's existence; it simply notes that only the fool says there is no God (Ps. 14:1). In the same way, nowhere in the Bible is Satan's existence proven. It assumes that people recognize Satan as real and that his reality is important. Satan is not portrayed as a mere metaphor or symbol of evil in Scripture; he is a created being who entices towards evil. His very name means "accuser," and it aptly describes him.

As a creature, he is limited, finite, and constrained by his Creator. He is not the sovereign, all-powerful being that Jennifer imagined. He owes his moment-by-moment existence to the continuing grace and mercy of God. Put simply: Satan is not equal to God. Christianity is not a dualistic religion, a faith in which two opposing but equal powers struggle for control. Even so, many Christians live as though Satan were as powerful as God. They rightly fear him, but they allow that fear to paralyze them. An African proverb says, "When the elephants fight, the grass gets trampled." In practical terms, many Christians live as though this were an accurate picture of spiritual warfare. God is battling Satan, and you and I are the blades of grass getting trampled in the process.

Nothing could be further from the truth! God is sovereign and all-powerful. Nowhere in the Bible do we see God engaged in a direct fight with Satan, as if he were an equal foe. The closest we get is Revelation 19, which describes Christ's triumphant slaughter of God's enemies who have gathered to do battle against him. Because God is sovereign, Satan does not stand a chance.

Engaging the Truth
➤ *What is your present view of Satan? How does it differ from what the Bible states?*
➤ *How does Satan entice us to believe he is all-powerful?*

Satan Is a Tempter

It appears that at least a part of God's original design in creating Satan, even before he became a fallen creature and enemy of God, was that he test or sift our intentions. This function is glimpsed in Luke 22:31-32. Jesus tells the disciple Simon Peter, "Satan has asked to sift you as wheat. But I have prayed for you, Simon, that your faith may not fail. And when you have turned back, strengthen your brothers."

In his pride Satan went beyond his role as sifter, beyond God's intention, and became a destroyer and a murderer. This underscores the essence of sin: taking something good that God has given and stretching it beyond its intended boundaries. Satan's work as a sifter/destroyer may be seen as a spectrum of roles linked to biblical terms (see figure 2), each role moving progressively closer to his ultimate goal of death and destruction.

Satan is the tester. His concentration on tempting us to disobey God is persistent. Luke says that once Jesus faced him down, Satan left for a "more opportune time" (Luke 4:13). It is this kind of persistence that enables Satan to be so successful in leading the world astray.

Satan is also an *accuser,* bringing his accusations about us

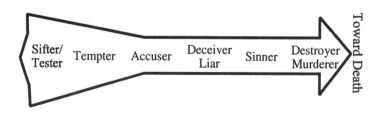

Figure 2
The Spectrum of Satan's Character

before God as well as hitting us with them as hard as he can. For me, often there is no hint of accusation when I'm actually being tempted, but once I give in, there is a constant drone of "You can't really be a Christian and do that!" He's a pro at piling on the guilt and shame with his taunts and false charges.

Engaging the Truth
➤ *In what ways have you felt "sifted" or accused by Satan recently? How have you responded?*
➤ *What might be the benefits of viewing these times as opportunities that God allows?*

Satan Is a Liar

Satan's temptation strategy is to mix truth with lies. In the Garden, he told Eve that eating the forbidden fruit would make her like God in that she would know good and evil. He failed to remind her that she would learn of evil by becoming evil herself in her disobedience. Similarly, he showed Jesus the kingdoms of the world in all their glory, saying that the short cut to gaining them was to worship Satan. By focusing on the kingdoms' glitter, Satan tried to hide their sinfulness. He paints a bright face on disobedience, conveniently leaving out the consequences, and God gives us the freedom to make our choice.

In philosophical terms, to define a lie we must be able to define truth. If there were no truth, there could be no such thing as a lie, just as counterfeit money would have no meaning unless real money existed and had value. A lie needs a reference point in order to be identified as a lie. Lies are not always the opposite of truth, but they are always distortions of it. The same can be said of evil. By definition, evil is dependent on the existence of good.

Philosophers call this a *contingent* existence, since evil is contingent on the existence of good for its own definition. *Good* does not need evil to be defined; it is founded in God's character. Evil, on the other hand, is a perversion and distortion of what is good, just as a lie is a perversion of the truth.

Telling a lie is not a creative act, but a *dis*-creative act. Thus Satan himself is a *dis*-creative being. His facility as a liar is dependent on his ability to start from truth, then distort it. The best lies are not outright contradictions of truth but subtle distortions of it, just as the best counterfeit money looks and feels like the real thing. Lying can be placed on a spectrum of stretching the truth to outright contradiction of truth. To use a special-effects term, Satan "morphs" truth as far as we let him (see figure 3). The subtle lie, intermingled with truth, is his greatest weapon in turning Christians away from the Creator.

Engaging the Truth
➤ *Can you identify some way Satan has distorted truth in your life? Why was it so appealing to you?*
➤ *How can you defend yourself against his subtle but powerful techniques?*

Satan Is Crafty

Genesis 3:1 notes that the "serpent was more crafty than any of the wild animals the Lord God had made." The main issue here is not that of a literal snake but that Satan was indeed the power behind the temptation. In this account, we see several aspects of his craftiness. When talking to Eve, he acted as though he were startled at God's command. By misstating the command as a prohibition against eating from all trees, he took the generous provision of God and turned Eve's focus on the one limitation. He brought Eve to the point where she felt that she had to defend God.

He also used a good goal to lead her on. He offered Eve a short

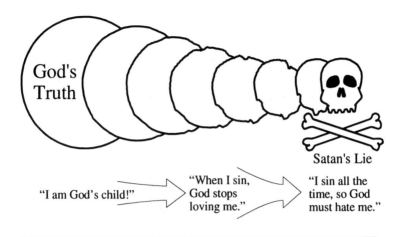

Figure 3
Satan's Transformation of Truth

cut to be like God: all she had to do was disobey him and act on her own. Being conformed to God's image is our destiny, something for which our hearts naturally strive. Satan convinced Eve to believe that taking the fruit that God prohibited was the path to her goal. The battle was won.

In Jesus' temptation, the devil took a promise of God ("He will command his angels concerning you, and they will lift you up in their hands, so that you will not strike your foot against a stone.") and enticed Jesus to use it as a cheap formula to put demands on God. Satan knows Scripture and is more than willing to use it for his own ends. But Jesus saw the offer for what it was.

The evil one takes advantage of our ability to think and capitalizes on our propensity for reasoning our way into doing something we know is wrong. He is delighted to point us toward a good goal and encourage us to take a short cut to reach it. He is also delighted when he can lead us to substitute good goals with lesser ones, hoping that he can begin a cycle that leads us towards self-destruction. And underneath every one of his actions is the driving desire to get our eyes off of God.

Engaging the Truth
➤ *What are some ways you have been tempted to take short cuts in developing godly character?*
➤ *Do you find yourself rationalizing about sin in your life or justifying the means to a wrong end? How can you fight these mental spiritual battles?*

Satan Wants to Be God

Ultimately, Satan is not satisfied with taking our eyes off God. In the end, he wants them clearly focused on himself. He is like a thief who wants to steal for himself the honor and allegiance we rightfully owe to our Creator. In tempting Eve, he presented himself as the one who had the inside scoop on what God was really thinking. He impugned God's character and presented God as a deceptive liar. He projected his own character onto God, and Eve bought the lie. Rather than thinking through the implications of what Satan said, she looked at the fruit from his evil perspective. It was a simple step from there to rationalize that the fruit actually would be good for her.

By presenting himself as the one who really cared—and by painting God as a jealous creature who did not want to share his best possessions—Satan successfully enticed Eve to honor him instead. The evil one wants to multiply that success in every human heart and thereby establish a kingdom for himself (Matt. 4:8-9; Col. 1:13). This dominion, by nature, is temporary and counterfeit, a place in which the Creator is replaced by a creature. It is a kingdom of deception, domination, and destruction.

Engaging the Truth
➤ *How is it helpful in your daily life to know more about who Satan is?*
➤ *What are ways you can recognize Satan's attempts to replace God's place in your heart?*

Satan Is at War

Satan is jealous of every human being because we are what
he can never be: beings made in the image of God. Knowing
that a direct frontal assault on God himself is doomed, he
focuses his energy on those made in God's image, particularly
Christians.

In this battle we should note that Satan's authority, power, and
control are contingent. His rebellion amounts to nothing unless
we participate; he is dependent on us. The more we believe his
lies, the greater his power over us. The more we spread discord
and live destructively, the greater his ability to influence us and
those around us. As Heinrich Schlier has noted, "Christ has left
the devil only whatever power our unbelief allows him."[1] Hence,
our goal is to *dis*believe in Satan[2] in the sense that we do not fall
for his lies. We believe *about* and *against* him rather than
believing *in* him.[3]

Engaging the Truth
➤ *What, to you, is the difference between believing in Satan and*
   believing against him?
➤ *How does knowing you are made in God's image put spiritual*
   warfare into better perspective?

Satan Is a Destroyer

While Satan's ultimate goal is our literal destruction ("He was a
murderer from the beginning," Jesus says in John 8:44), he
moves toward that goal by figuratively murdering, or destroying,
our relationships with God, others, and ourselves. He takes
pleasure in broken relationships marked by betrayal, abuse,
bullying, apathy, jealousy, and emotional bondage. He takes
pleasure in people who are so driven by hurt, anger, and bitterness that these emotions become the foundation for their

relationships with others. Why else would he be interested in two small human beings in the Garden of Eden? Why else would he be so bent on thwarting God's purposes in the wilderness with Jesus? There's no indication that Satan felt anything during these temptations. He wages war and destruction with no conscience.

Engaging the Truth
➤ *What does it mean to "murder" a relationship in the figurative sense?*
➤ *How has Satan tried to use broken relationships in your life in destructive ways?*

Satan Is Doomed

In the Genesis temptation story, Satan is the first character to be judged by God: "Cursed are you above all . . . the animals! You will crawl on your belly and you will eat dust all the days of your life" (Gen. 3:14). In other words, Satan will be humbled and humiliated by God. God also stated that Satan would engage in a battle with Eve's descendants ("you will strike his heel") but would be defeated ("he will crush your head," vs. 15). This defeat was established through Jesus' death on the cross. We participate in it as we live to please God because of our trust in Christ's work.

Satan's final reward for his work, together with his demonic hosts, is hell (Matt. 25:41). In Revelation 20 we see the completion of God's pronouncement. Satan is bound and cast into an abyss for one thousand years, and then tossed into the lake of fire. It takes no battle to subdue him, only God's desire that it be done. The Bible keeps Satan in his proper place—and our focus on God—by stating this final event as a settled issue. No discussion, no debate. This is good news! The enemy of our souls, who can look so powerful to us, stands as a defeated foe. And our task is to live in light of his defeat.

Engaging the Truth
➤ *What is your response to the fact that the evil one is ultimately doomed?*
➤ *How does this reality encourage you in daily struggles?*

Satan in the Church?

It should not surprise us that, according to a recent survey from the Barna Group, nearly half of the people questioned felt that Satan is not real at all, but only a means of expressing the reality of evil.[4] It *should* surprise us, however, that this survey was conducted among those associated with evangelical churches. Any Christians who do not believe that Satan is real will be ill-equipped to develop a church community that reflects God's order to the world.

Of course, those who believe in the evil one's existence are not automatically free from deception. Many carry their belief too far, placing satanic workers in the heart of every church. One young woman told me that the louder people praise God, the less she trusts them. This came out of her own experience in facing church leaders who were abusive. Another told me that she knew some of the elders of a local church were closet Satanists; a friend had been abused and had pointed the finger at them. Some conspiracy-driven books suggest that the church is a rat's nest of hidden satanic activities.

All of this plays into Satan's desire to be seen as everywhere and able to do anything he wants. Spiritual warfare is not believing that he is everywhere but recognizing that wherever he is, God holds the leash. Some churches may have been infiltrated by those who have given their allegiance to Satan, but even Satanists can come to Christ!

What about Demons?

As we saw in chapter 3, when Jesus encountered the demoniac, he asked the name of the demon holding the man captive. The demon's response was, "My name is Legion, for we are many" (Mark 5:9). The Bible clearly teaches that Satan is not alone in his attack on humanity. He leads an army of demons who do the bulk of his dirty work. Before we go too far into this discussion, though, we should note that the Bible, in contrast to other writings from ancient times, rarely mentions the activities of these other spirits. Generally speaking, they are not discussed theologically but are presented as actors in concrete events, their nature being seen by their actions. Most scholars today recognize them as angels who fell with Satan and who are in league with him.

The spirit activities we encounter in the Old Testament are connected to the idols and idolatry of the nations as well as to the gods served by those nations: "They sacrificed to demons, which are not God—gods they had not known, gods that recently appeared, gods your fathers did not fear" (Deut. 32:17). Evil spirits may even be sent by God as a judgment on individuals for personal sin (1 Sam. 16:14) or as a judgment on entire local populations for corporate sin (Judg. 9:23-24). They are organized in some form of hierarchy, but we are left without any details of how it works. Perhaps the most striking aspect of the Old Testament discussion is that spirits do not act as independent agents. Sent by God as judgment, as seen in the above examples, they operate under his control and move at his bidding.

In the New Testament there is a dramatic increase in quantity and clarity of encounters with evil spirits. They are described as wicked and unclean; agents of Satan who participate in his rebellious works and share his destiny. Not surprisingly, they are more active during Jesus' life than at any other time in the Bible.

The most detailed confrontations between Jesus and evil spirits are his encounter with the demoniac (Mark 5:1-20) and the freeing of a boy with seizures (Mark 9:14-29). In addition, the Gospels include three reports of people being healed of diseases caused by spirits, and two in which the spirits are silenced (see Matt. 9:32-33; 12:22-23; Luke 13:10-17; and Mark 1:23-27; Luke 4:40-41). Even though we see what may appear to be many different encounters, in many cases Gospel writers are telling the same story from a slightly different perspective. Not including the general statements (that "those with demons were healed"), altogether there are less than ten distinct occasions of direct demonic confrontation by Jesus, all scattered over the three years of his public ministry.

When compared with the Gospels, the book of Acts and the Epistles contain relatively few reports of demonic encounters. Only five instances are recorded in Acts (5:15-16; 8:6-7; 16:16-18; 19:11-12, 13-17). In the Epistles, we do find foundational teaching on spirits and their activities. For example, Paul warns that demons blind the minds of unbelievers (2 Cor. 4:3-4). He also shows that they play on our physical appetites in hopes of shifting our attention to the exclusive pursuit of pleasure or sensual gratification and that they are the power behind religious idolatry (1 Cor. 10:19-21; Eph. 5:6; Col. 2:8; 2 Thess. 2:3). John indicates that the spirits are to be tested rather than accepted for whatever they claim and that spirits influence by leading people astray from truth (1 John 4:1-4; Rev. 12:9).

Demon Control

Several words in the original language of the Bible are used to describe the range of demonic attacks on people. Demons are able to *indwell* or control a person, just as Christ and the Spirit indwell Christians. Along the same lines, people may have spirits *in* them, or be *with* a spirit, or *have* spirits. Though the vocabulary of spirit attacks against people is rich and varied, it is all focused on the demons' desire to drive people to live in a way that violates their image of God. Demons, like their master, desire our destruction. See appendix C for a list of several passages describing demonic attacks.

The ultimate biblical term of control is *demonized.* This term is often translated as "demon possessed," which adds an unfortunate English connotation of literal ownership. However, in the original language, ownership or eternal destiny is not the intended meaning. *Control* is at the heart of the issue. *The Amplified Bible* captures it well with a translation of "under the power of demons."

Interestingly, the term *exorcism* is not used in the New Testament concerning the early church's ministry. The word itself means "to command by use of an oath or formula." Typically, then, an exorcism involves a ritual. Jesus, as well as the early church, relied on authority rather than ritual.

Stay Alert

In Ephesians 2:2, Paul relates that Satan is "at work in the lives of those who are disobedient." This is not to say that all unbelievers are demonized. Rather, it indicates that the very air they breathe, as it were, is tainted by Satan's control over them. The particular vehicles he uses are the same as in the Garden of Eden, namely, the lusts and desires of both flesh and mind. God is the Creator of both flesh and mind, but Satan twists them to his own ends in the lives of those who walk apart from Christ.

In light of Satan's nature and character, it is no wonder that Jennifer, Martha, and Tim all had distorted views of him and his demonic hosts. These deceivers are willing to wear any disguise necessary to distort our view of the truth. Jennifer needed to recognize that God's sovereignty is unchallenged and reject the lie that Satan is all-powerful. Martha needed to understand that

Satan is a real being and that his goal is her destruction. Tim needed to see that Satan leaves alone only those who are comfortably in his grip. In what ways do you need to bring your views of the enemy more in line with truth?

Satan is not a mere symbol of evil, not a comical character wearing red tights and carrying a pitchfork, and not a true challenger to God. He is simply a creature who has chosen a path of rebellion and destruction in a futile attempt to overthrow the One who made him. While we are not to attribute every temptation to him, neither are we to think that he and his minions are simply sitting by, idly waiting for us to fall. We need to be aware and alert and know the enemy so that we can stand firm against his attacks.

6

Who Are the Targets?

I met Jim one summer while working on a beach-evangelism project. Friendly and fun to be with, in addition to being a varsity athlete at a major university, he always seemed to have a crowd of people surrounding him. More important, Jim was a committed Christian and a bold evangelist not afraid to share his faith with anyone. He apparently had it all together. But a week before I was scheduled to return home, Jim wanted to talk with me. We sat down, and he pulled a piece of paper out of his pocket, saying that he had been working on this for a while and wanted me to see it. It was a list of thirty-nine things that he hated about himself. In spite of his outward success in sports, the ease with which he made friends, and his love for Christ, he was convinced he had nothing to offer. He felt trapped in habits that he had grown to hate. Satan's arrows had hit the target.

Reacting instinctively, I told him that he should be glad he didn't see God's list, which probably had thirty-nine hundred things on it. The look on his face told me he was listening! I reminded him that Christ had taken that entire list to the cross. Jesus knew every item on the list, every intimate detail of Jim's life, and still loved him enough to die for him. The feelings Jim had about himself were suddenly brought into perspective. He had been seeking to connect with God through performance, but he was dissatisfied with his ability to perform well enough. As a result, he derided himself because he felt insignificant in light of his performance. Jim had defined himself in terms of what he *did* rather than *who he was*. He had been the target of negative attacks of the enemy because he had lost sight of the truth.

Jim's mistake was a common one, especially for Americans. Ask us who we are, and we will tell you what we do. When we do well, we feel good about ourselves. When we perform poorly or try to compare ourselves to others who are better performers, we stop feeling good. Satan is out to destroy all of God's creation, especially human beings. If we do not have a clear sense of our identity as God's created beings, we will be an easy target for Satan's lies.

So, what does the Bible tell us about our identity and who we are as human beings? We will turn again to the opening chapters of Genesis for insights that are true of all human beings. Then we will focus more specifically on those who are Christians and look at selected insights on spiritual warfare from the New Testament epistles. Though there are no specific questions for reflection in this chapter, I again invite you to prayerfully reflect on the implications of each truth for spiritual warfare in your life.

We Are Created by God

"The Lord God formed man from the dust of the ground, and breathed into his nostrils the breath of life" (Gen. 2:7, NRSV). God is the Creator, and we are the created ones. We are the direct result of the personal expression of his eternal significance. He designed us and knows best how we are to live.

God made us *physical* beings. As creatures with physical bodies, we have the basic appetites for the necessities of existence: air, food, water, shelter, and procreation. They are God-given and therefore good. However, they must be recognized for what they are: appetites that may be satisfied for a season but that will always return.

From a spiritual warfare perspective, the two most readily abused physical areas are our sexual drive and our need for food. These appetites must be satisfied within the guidelines of God's divinely ordained order, an order that Satan seeks to distort. Sexual distortions deny God's intention that sex be a source of pleasure, intimacy, and procreation within the marriage relationship, and misuses of sex can range from lust-driven thinking to bestiality. Eating distortions deny the Creator's intention for food to be a pleasurable source of nourishment to sustain life and to honor our bodies as God's creation. They range from an undisciplined diet to severe eating disorders. (This is not to say that the underlying emotions are sin, but the continuous acting out of self-destructive habits can be sin.)

We have been created to glorify God—to give allegiance to, to honor, and to acknowledge him in the way we live. Whatever you place at the center of your existence is what you have chosen to glorify. Even though we were created to glorify God, every time we sin, we in effect glorify (or give allegiance to, honor, and acknowledge) Satan. No wonder God treats sin so seriously! Every act of sin is an act of rebellion, even treason, against God himself. This idea is seen in Romans 6, where Paul tells us to choose whom we will serve, sin or God. The choice is not *whether* we serve but *whom* we serve.

We Bear God's Image

Not only are we created beings, we are created in God's image (Gen. 1:26-27). Nothing else in all creation shares this attribute, not even the angels. This fact makes humanity significant in God's sight solely because of *who we are*. Theologians have argued for centuries over the meaning and significance of the *imago dei*. We will not solve those questions here. Our goal simply is to look at several of the implications of this truth that are important for spiritual warfare.

Our lives have purpose.
In the Garden of Eden, Adam and Eve were commissioned to fill the earth and subdue it (Gen. 1:28). They were to serve as visible agents of God's rule over the created order. In their service they displayed God's image by exercising authority in just and loving ways. They were not significant because they were entrusted with dominion; rather, they were entrusted with dominion *because they were significant.*

Because we are made in God's image, we find our deepest meaning and purpose in that we are *by nature* significant. This discovery has been very helpful to me in fighting spiritual battles in various areas of my life. I'm learning not to think of myself as *becoming* significant because of what I accomplish. Instead, I can *experience* the significance I already have by faithfully serving Christ. I am able to do this because of who God has made me to be through Christ's work on my behalf.

On the darker side, many people feel significant because of the power they hold over others. This applies not only to those in political power but also to those who victimize others. These people are bearing God's image in an ungodly fashion. That is one of the reasons that power corrupts. Without corresponding godliness, power always dominates and eventually leads to destruction.

We are spiritual beings.
Another aspect of being created in God's image is that we are spiritual beings. Our destiny is to be like God, conformed to the likeness of his Son (Romans 8:29). As spiritual creatures, nothing should get us more excited than being conformed to Jesus' likeness! Also, as spiritual creatures, we are susceptible to the influence of other spiritual creatures (whether human or demonic). Our lives will be permeated by some form of spirituality.

We are psychological beings.
We are not only physical and spiritual beings; we are also

psychological—thinking, choosing, and feeling people. We are endowed with these capacities to enable us to find new and creative ways to develop intimacy with our Creator. When Adam named the animals in Genesis 2, he was exercising his God-given abilities to think, create, and choose what to call each one. Emotions were also part of the process, as with a child who delights in exploring his or her world. At the same time, as a result of our sin, Satan wants to use these very same capacities to alienate us from God.

As *thinking* beings, God wants us to know, understand, and correctly interpret the truth. We have the ability to reason. Satan would have us ignore, distort, or deny the truth. We also have the capacity to *choose* and are responsible for our choices. Adam and Eve were given clear instructions and then left alone by God to face the temptation to consider going their own way. Satan's purposes are served when we forget the fact that we always have choices. We will expand on this aspect of spiritual warfare later in this chapter.

We are also *feeling* beings who experience a full range of God-given emotions. God desires that we become aware of our feelings and handle them appropriately. Satan is pleased when we deny or suppress emotions or when we allow them to control our actions. He is happy with either extreme of "feelings are everything" or "no feelings at all."

Michelle, who had been abused as a child, buried her anger and shame for years. As we talked, she began to realize that she would have to reconnect with her feelings. This stopped her cold; she was not ready. Several months later I saw her again, and her countenance was completely changed. She had found a friend who was willing to walk with her through the process of opening the door to all of the agonizing emotions she had shoved down deep inside. Though painful, working through these feelings was the beginning of her healing. Today she continues the process, and she is growing in her relationship with God as a result.

We are social and cultural beings.

After Adam finished his work of naming the animals, something was still missing (Gen. 2:18, 20). Even though Adam experienced a direct relationship with God, he needed a human partner to work with him and share his world. God created Eve to serve this purpose. God has made us all with basic social needs. People inescapably *need* other people. We need fellowship, friendship, and intimacy that can only be found in our relating to other people. In creating Eve, God laid the foundation for all cultures, which are built on language, interaction, and social rules and regulations.

As every human being has this need for relationship, it is one area that Satan targets whenever possible. Remember the discussion in chapter 1 of the five different fronts on which spiritual battle can be waged? Attacks in this relational area can easily affect us on several fronts: our personal lives, our relationships with each other, the unity of the local church, and even on the larger world systemic front. We will explore the implications of Satan's distortions and our struggle to know and apply truth at these levels more in the second and third sections of the book.

We are whole beings.

Made in God's image, we are whole and integrated beings. I am not just a psychological person, or a social person, or a spiritual person, or a physical person. I am not just a collection of those characteristics tossed together like a salad, but an integrated blending of them, all working together and all affecting each other. An African proverb states, "When you hit one part of the drum, the whole drum vibrates." In the same way, if you "strike" one part of me, it affects every other part of my being as well.

This has interesting implications for spiritual warfare. Many people ask how you can know if a problem is a psychological or spiritual one. From my experience, very few problems can be isolated to one of these areas. Further, by framing the question in that way, they leave out physical and cultural realities. Whatever our view of personhood, we must recognize that all of the above elements of being made in God's image come together as a whole and cannot be easily separated.

The spiritual factors of who we are undergird and permeate the other aspects of being human and should never be discounted. At the same time, however, they rarely (if ever) are apart from the total context of who we are physically, psychologically, socially, and culturally. I saw this clearly in a situation when I was teaching in Africa.

Japheth, a young man in Kenya, came to me convinced that his brother was "demonic." His proof? That the brother came home drunk one day, and Japheth started preaching at him about his drunkenness. The brother began hitting Japheth in response. Sometime later I went to Japheth's house to visit with an aunt, who he also claimed was demonized. The aunt and I had a delightful conversation, and I had the opportunity to share Christ with her. Just before leaving, Japheth showed me his room. On his desk was a book written by an author who holds that all forms of antagonism against Christians are demonic. Suddenly Japheth's world view became more clear to me. Though he himself was an extremely abrasive person who constantly antagonized others, this book had given Japheth permission to ignore his own personality problems and label all conflicts as "demonic." God intends for his truth to be applied in all areas of life. Japheth spiritualized the results of his own social abrasiveness and needed to look at his own life rather than blaming his problems on demons working in the lives of others.

We Have the Power of Choice

A truth that applies to all people is that we retain the ability to choose. We are free to choose good or to choose evil. Certainly one of the darkest times in human history was when Adam and

Eve ate of the forbidden tree. Wanting to be like God, they chose the ungodly path of disobedience. Because of their sin and our own participation in sin, our ability to connect with the godly image we bear is broken. While they could choose sin, Adam and Eve could *not* control the consequences of that choice, a principle that applies today as well.

One consequence of their choice is that we experience broken relationships. After Adam and Eve sinned, *they hid from each other,* seeing their nakedness for the first time. Today, we still hide from each other, afraid to let others see what is taking place inside of us. Adam and Eve *hid from God* in fear. We, too, run from him—or remake him in our own image—so we can feel good about ourselves and ignore the rift in our relationship. We may even deny God out of fear of being exposed and judged by those around us. Adam and Eve also *hid from themselves,* trying to shift the blame when confronted with what they had done. Adam blamed Eve (going so far as to blame *God* for giving her to him). Eve blamed the serpent. They each denied their own responsibility. We hide from ourselves too, refusing to search out our own hearts for fear of what we might find. Yet we are too ready to find blame in others.

This truth was forcefully brought home to me one day when I got confused about the time of a welcoming party given for me. My wife and I showed up at my boss's house three hours early. I was extremely embarrassed, and my embarrassment turned to anger as we got in the car to return home. Do you know what I wanted to do? I wanted to find a way to blame my wife for my mistake and embarrassment! I could feel the mental wheels turning as I churned through the ways I could accuse her. She looked at me, knowing the inner struggle, and said, "Just remember, God is in charge." That was what I needed to hear, though it took close to an hour for it to sink in. When we later made the trip to the party, God had ministered to me through her words, but not without a struggle on my part. Like Adam, I try to hide things from myself and shift the blame on others. I, too, am a creature of broken relationships. Thankfully, though, this is not the end of the story!

Because we have been given the power of choice, human beings can also choose godliness. Repeatedly in the Old Testament we are told to exercise this ability. When the Israelites had entered the Promised Land, Joshua exhorted them, "Fear the Lord and serve him will all faithfulness. . . . But if serving the Lord seems undesirable to you, then choose for yourselves this day whom you will serve" (Josh. 24:14-15). In the New Testament, we are invited to respond to Christ: "If anyone is thirsty, let him come to me and drink" (John 7:37). Even in the midst of our sin, we can choose Christ. In spite of Satan's best efforts, no human being ever fully loses this ability to choose God's way. Many deny they have it, or feel so trapped that they do not know how to exercise it. By the power of God's work in human hearts, however, there is hope for every person to be able to come to Christ. And when we have so chosen, what does our identity in Christ mean in terms of spiritual warfare?

Spiritual Warfare Truths about Followers of Christ

Spiritual warfare is not an idea or term born in the twentieth century. It began when Adam and Eve chose a path of destruction. Their ancient choice put all of humanity, and particularly Christians, in the midst of spiritual battle. We are promised that the struggle between God and the evil one will continue until Satan is finally defeated. Paul alludes to this in his statement to the Christians at Rome: "The God of peace will soon crush Satan under your feet" (Rom. 16:20). You and I, as part of Christ's church, through the power of God, will crush the enemy. We do not need to go out and attack Satan; he is more than ready to come after us. We cannot escape the reality of the battle if we are to grow in our relationship with Christ. But we are assured that God will win the overall and ultimate victory. As believers, we are equipped with some important truths for standing firm until then.

We have a new identity.

One central theme of spiritual warfare in the Bible is that of our new identity in Christ. This identity—a new definition of who we are—is absolutely foundational for being equipped for battle on all fronts. To deal with this topic further, let's go to the New Testament.

Through the apostle Paul's ministry, many people living in the great city of Ephesus had come to follow Christ. In the first century A.D., Ephesus was a city with a reputation for great magic and access to spiritual powers. If ever there was a people in the heat of spiritual battle, it was the Ephesians. These new Christians did not run away from the spiritually oppressive atmosphere of the city. Paul knew that they would be tempted to return to the old ways of magical protection to meet the needs of life. So he composed a letter as a primer to help the Ephesians deal with real-life spiritual warfare.

Nearly half of Paul's letter is spent grounding his readers in the truth of the gospel. One of the ringing themes in the epistle is what had been granted to the Ephesians by virtue of the fact that they now were "in Christ." In Ephesians 1:3-14, which originally was one very long sentence, Paul points out all the blessings God has given. He uses the phrase *in Christ* no less than seven times in this one sentence. Paul's point? To encourage the Ephesian Christians with the idea that God has blessed his people with every spiritual blessing in Christ. We were chosen and predestined to be adopted in him. Through our hope in him we have redemption and forgiveness of sins, having been included and marked with the Spirit.

But Paul does not end there. In Ephesians 2 and 3, he states that we have been raised with Christ and seated in the heavenly realms in him. God's kindness to us is expressed in Christ, and we are created in Christ to do good works. The Ephesians, who were once far away from God, have been brought near in Christ. Through him, all believers have free access to God—Jews and Gentiles alike. He reminded the Ephesians that God's purpose was to use the church to show the "heavenly authorities" (that is, Satan and the spirits aligned with him) the extent of God's wonderful wisdom, grace, and mercy.

We are new people.
In 2 Corinthians 5:17, Paul declares that everyone who is in Christ "is a new creation; the old has gone, the new has come!" The moment you came to Christ in faith, through the power of God's Spirit, you were transformed into a new person. You "were dead in your transgressions and sins" and are now "alive with Christ" (Eph. 2:1, 5).

It is also true that we have yet to experience completely what this transformation means. Our new life is a two-sided process, similar to what the kingdom of God is in society. While the kingdom *has come,* it is also still *in the process of coming* and will finally be fully revealed. We live in the tension of the "already, but not yet." Like a chick hatching from an egg, we are in process. We have already experienced much—but much more is still to come!

We are saints in Christ.
Most of us feel somewhat strange claiming, "I am a saint." Anyone who dares to declare it must be either crazy or conceited, we think. But the simple truth is that, in the New Testament, *all* Christians are called "saints." The word is not reserved only for those who supposedly live sinless, self-sacrificial lives, as our popular culture tells us. It is God's name for us. We are simply referring to ourselves as "ones who have been set apart by God for his purposes." We have been declared holy only as a result of Christ's work on our behalf—not because we are good in ourselves.

We are works in process.

Paul told the Corinthians that as believers, we *are being* transformed into Christ's likeness (2 Cor. 3:18). This continuing
sanctification in our lives is God's side of the work. Meanwhile,
the Christians in Rome were commanded to be transformed by
"renewing their minds" (Rom. 12:2). This is our side of the work.
The final step of the transformation will come when Christ "will
transform our lowly bodies so that they will be like his glorious
body" (Phil. 3:21).

Thus we are both passive recipients of and active partici-
pants in God's spiritual transforming work in our lives. The
transformation will not be complete until we see God face
to face. It is this change towards Christlikeness that Satan
fears and hates the most about us. As we become more and
more like Christ, we remind the evil one that he is no longer
our master.

We are designed for eternity.

While we may face difficult battles now, we will not face them
forever. As fierce and long as spiritual warfare on earth may get
(and for some it costs their very lives), when compared to
eternity it is not even a blip on the screen. Consider this: The
Gospel of Luke tells us that on one occasion, Jesus sent the
disciples out to engage the enemy (Luke 10:1-20). When they
returned, they were delighted that the demons had submitted to
them. But Jesus put it all in perspective for them: "Do not rejoice
that the spirits submit to you, but rejoice that your names are
written in heaven." Spiritual warfare is a temporary state for the
Christian; living with Christ is an eternal one.

We Are Members of a Community

There is no doubt that God calls us to faith as individuals and
that we wage spiritual warfare as individuals. At the same time,

there is no doubt that God calls us to be part of a community in which we put others' needs ahead of our own.

> If you have any encouragement from being united with Christ, if any comfort from his love, if any fellowship with the Spirit, if any tenderness and compassion, then make my joy complete by being like-minded, having the same love, being one in spirit and purpose. Do nothing out of selfish ambition or vain conceit, but in humility consider others better than yourselves. Each of you should look not only to your own interests, but also to the interests of others. (Phil. 2:1-4)

Here, Paul rightly assumes that we can look out for our own interests. But he calls us to also commit ourselves to looking out for the interests of others. The model for this attitude was Christ himself, who did not grasp after that which was rightfully his but surrendered himself to God for our sake.

The Vineyard Christian Fellowship of Cincinnati, Ohio, is one church that has taken this call to others-living seriously. To reach out to the greater Cincinnati community, the church began a "conspiracy of kindness," engaging in random acts of kindness to people in the city. These acts were simple—yet visible and practical—expressions of Christ's unconditional love intended as an evangelistic outreach. They ranged from giving away Cokes at stoplights to raking leaves to cleaning toilets—all with no strings attached. The result? The church is one of the fastest growing churches in the United States, exploding from the initial Sunday attendance of 37 to over 2,500 seven years later![1]

God created us from the very beginning to be members of a community. As I noted earlier, people are social creatures; we exist in the context of relationships. We were not made to be alone; we are to live in fellowship with God and with God's people. The church is the place of God's community focus. It consists of those who have been called out of the world into

God's kingdom. It is not a building but the people themselves who make up the church. It is comprised not of all people but of only those whom God has called out to be his children.

In the New Testament there are several images denoting the collective nature of the church: we are the bride of Christ, the body of Christ, the temple of God, and the sheep of Christ the Shepherd. Each picture is one of life, vitality, and growth in the context of being part of something larger than ourselves. As the bride, we are preparing for our marriage to Christ. As the body, we are his visible expression of love to a dying world. As the temple of God, each of us is a stone being used to build the house in which God himself lives. As the sheep of the Shepherd, we know his voice and follow his leading. We exist as a church to glorify our Creator, not to be enslaved to an institution.

We Are Members of a Kingdom

Another amazing truth about who we are as Christians is our new citizenship. Through Christ, we have been delivered from the kingdom of darkness and transferred into the kingdom of light. Now we are citizens of heaven. God's kingdom is his continued and eternal rule over creation made by and for him. In contrast to other kingdoms, it is eternal. God alone brings it to pass, and it will spread despite our rejection, for it is God's intention that it be universal. Its value cannot be measured—it is worth all we have and are, and its rewards are determined by God's sovereign grace. While the "old country" does try to reclaim our citizenship, we have been given new papers and new lives suitable for our new kingdom. We can consider ourselves dead to the old ways.

As human beings we are embedded in the cultural systems around us. Sin is not limited to the individual—it has affected systems as well, changing the very social structures through which we live our lives. In fact, as much as we sin individually, our tendency toward sin is compounded in cultural systems. Thus, all cultures are not just tainted but *inhabited* by sin. Spiritual warfare at this cultural level requires that we confront the culture everywhere it is bent away from God and encourage its return to the Creator. The 1982 Lausanne Committee report on "Evangelism and Social Responsibility" offers some guidelines for what this kind of kingdom living can look like:

> First, the new community should constitute a challenge to the old. Its values and ideals, its moral standards and relationships, its sacrificial life-style, its love, joy and peace—these are the signs of the Kingdom . . . and present the world with a radically alternative society.
>
> Secondly, as the world lives alongside the Kingdom community, some of the values of the Kingdom spill over into society as a whole, so that its industry, commerce, legislation and institutions become to some degree imbued with Kingdom values.

The heavenly kingdom to which we belong is at war with the world in which we physically live. We are targets of a persistent and sly enemy. Everywhere we turn, the enemy seeks to subjugate, distort, and deny the reality of God's encroaching kingdom. But like a child with its finger in the hole of a bursting dike, Satan's attempts to hold God's kingdom at bay are futile. We can powerfully resist the enemy with the weapons God has provided: truth, confession and repentance, forgiveness, extending blessings for cursings, and loving our enemies. This is the core of spiritual warfare.

In conclusion, how might this kind of kingdom living be fleshed out in real life?

On the *personal front:* Follow kingdom priorities, make godly decisions, and live like a "saint" called out for God's glory. Be aware of and expose Satan's deception in your life and cooperate with God in the process of transforming you into the image of his Son, Jesus.

On the *interpersonal front:* Appreciate and encourage others in your life, exhort each other, pray for each other, and minister to each other.

On the *front of the local church:* Work for unity, support holy living, and allow an atmosphere where the spiritual gifts can operate freely.

On the larger *systemic front:* Endeavor to recognize and combat the ways our popular culture herds you away from God into worldly living or into apathetic faith.

This kind of living is a tall order. But we have been created by a great God who will strengthen and empower us. Let us shine as lights in our culture and act as salt to preserve the elements of godly character found in it.

II.
Spiritual Warfare
Disciplines

7

Unmasking Our Sin

We live in a culture of perceived control and convenience. We expect instant data, healthy fast-food dinners, immediate service, newer products, and faster results. The notion of delayed gratification appears to have died a gradual death in our society, and we run around whining like children when things don't go our way. I purposefully say "we" because I all too often want or demand instant results, even in spiritual maturity. I don't want to wait for patience or grow into it; I want to *have* patience now! For almost two thousand years, however, the church has recognized that the Christian life is a life of discipline.

The Classic Christian Disciplines

Our spiritual life is like a marathon in some ways, though many of us wish it were a simple sprint. We race from conference to conference, seeking the "keys" to growth, "secrets" of the Christian life, "steps to success," "how-tos" of successful marriages; the list is endless.

While conferences and retreats can offer refreshment, renewal, and recharging, life as a whole is not a high-intensity conference but a long, paced journey. There are no instant short cuts to full Christlike maturity, though God at times gives us quantum leaps in our development. The path of life as a whole is better pictured as a pilgrimage than a race. Spiritual growth is a measured transformation wrought through the cooperation of the human and the divine in the process of purging that which is ungodly and instilling that which reflects godliness.

This, in essense, is a description of the classic Christian spiritual disciplines. The purpose of the disciplines is not to somehow make us look better or more spiritual but to enable us to reflect on what is happening on the inside. They give us space to grow and give God space in our lives to bring the growth into being. The disciplines include *prayer, confession and repentance, praise and worship, and joyfully giving of our time, talents, and treasures.* The disciplines provide a way to regularly "strip off" the old sinful habits and "put on" the new clothes of godliness. They ground us in God's grace, even when the accuser comes.

Exposing the Accuser

Jesus is teaching in the temple courts when a group of religious leaders come to him, dragging a woman along with them. They shout their accusations: "Teacher, this woman was caught in the act of adultery. In the Law Moses commanded us to stone such women. Now what do you say?" (John 8:3-5).

You can feel their anticipation at the same time that you sense the woman's total shame and fear. Yet Jesus does not give in to their persistent needling. He stoops to write something in the dirt on the ground. We do not know what he wrote, but some have speculated that it may have been the names of the women with whom these men had committed adultery! In any event, Jesus' response is simple: "If any one of you is without sin, let him be the first to throw a stone at her."

One by one they slink away, shamed and reminded of their own sinfulness. After the last one leaves, Jesus asks the woman, "Where are [your accusers]? Has no one condemned you?" She replies, "No one, sir." Then Jesus declares, "Then neither do I condemn you. Go now, and leave your life of sin." He does not deny the reality of her sin, minimize its importance, or ignore its consequences. He forgives and exhorts her to turn her back on her sin.

This woman admitted to her sin before the crowd and Jesus. Her guilt was clear, viciously declared by her accusers, and she did not refute it. This "confession" became the vehicle for her to receive Jesus' forgiveness. What the teachers of the law and the Pharisees had meant for destruction, Jesus used for redemption.

We never hear about the man involved in her adultery. This is *her* story, the story of a woman who became a pawn in a scheme to attack and discredit Jesus before the people. Yet in God's loving and divine mercy, it is the victim alone who is granted release. Her unnamed male partner and the religious leaders are the losers, exposed for their hypocrisy and deceit.

Satan is the ultimate accuser (Rev. 12:10), and he loves to play the same role the religious leaders played. His strategy is to beat up on sinners, shame or humiliate them, accusing them over and over again. How many Christians in our churches are weighed down by sins that were disposed of on the Cross? How many carry unnecessary burdens because they do not understand the meaning of real grace? How many people have never experienced God's love through someone with whom they can confess their brokenness and gain acceptance and forgiveness? How many believers carry hidden hurts, afraid to confess them because they fear ostracism and condemnation?

In my own battle with lottery lust described earlier, I certainly felt accused by Satan as a failure. I resisted, but I found out that simply "driving Satan away" did nothing for *my* fears. That action of resistance, in and of itself, did not answer my needs for security and the desire I had (and still have) to provide for my family. It did not cause me to look at myself more honestly and ask what was really behind my lottery daydreams. This is because it focused all attention on Satan's work rather than my own lack of trust in God as the One who will provide for my needs. I needed to recognize not only that Satan was trying to take advantage of my insecurity but also, more foundationally, that *I was responsible before God for my unbelief.* I had to come to grips with my sin, just like the adulterous woman, if I was to find relief from my insecurities.

The Discipline of Repentance

In Romans 12:2, Paul tells believers to stop being conformed to the world and to be renewed in their minds. In Ephesians 4:22–5:2, he tells us to take off our old rags and put on new clothes. The author of Hebrews, using an athletic metaphor, encourages us to throw off everything that hinders us, "the sin that so easily entangles" (12:1). Nowhere, however, does Scripture say that replacing old, sinful ways with godly minds will be easy.

Wendell was a student of mine who came for some counsel. Originally he came to talk about his girlfriend, who was undergoing severe stress. But as we talked, he also mentioned that in the next few months he was going to have to "have it out" with his dad to see who would be in control of their home. It was obvious not only that the relationship was sour but also that Wendell had been deeply hurt by things his father had done. I asked Wendell if he would be willing to consider forgiving him. "No way!" he said, narrowing his eyes in anger. He had grown comfortable with the energy his hatred gave him, and he was not ready to release it. He was more than ready for his dad to repent, but unwilling to face his own need to do the same.

Imagine a burn patient who has to undergo the searing pain of having the dressings replaced. The searing pain of pulling the old dressings away from the damaged skin is almost unendurable. Without that agony, however, healing is impossible. How strongly we hold on to our old ways, how enmeshed we are in them, and how difficult it can be to shed them! Nevertheless, that is what God calls us to do, promising to replace our old, tattered, sinful clothes with fresh new clothes of righteousness appropriate for his children. This is not all God's work, and it is not all ours. Together we participate in the struggle to renew our minds. The first step in that renewal is getting rid of the old. Why is that so important? The reason lies in God's reaction to sin.

Let's Get Real

Sin is a flouting of who God is, a denial of his goodness and sovereignty as well as an assertion of human independence. Dan Allender and Tremper Longman, in their book *Bold Love,* call sin "hatred of God," pointing out that sin "is a defiant movement, sometimes unwitting and other times quite conscious, which refuses to depend on God for his direction and strength."[1]

Consider the story of Ananias and Sapphira in Acts 5:1-11, the couple who was struck dead for a seemingly "small" thing: misrepresenting the percentage of their income they had given to the church. (That God did not continue this radical pattern of judgment is another reminder of his mercy as it extends to our daily lives. I am glad that his mercy shields me!) But I am convinced that, under the Spirit's influence, Luke recorded the story of Ananias and Sapphira as a warning through the course of history that God does not play games with sin and will not downplay the significance of living holy lives before him.

I admit that I approach this whole topic of sin with some trepidation. On the most basic level, when I *repent,* I must honestly and openly admit to God the *reality of my sin* and my commitment *to turn away from that sin* by the power of God's Spirit working in me. I don't have difficulty with this root idea, but I am unable to see the depths of my need to repent. Humanly speaking, a truly accurate assessment of my need is an impossibility. It is not that I do not *want* to see this but that, as Jeremiah penned long ago, my heart is desperately wicked (Jer. 17:9). I so easily hide my sin from myself. Having a new nature and having been declared a saint by God, all too often I want to pretend that the "old Scott Moreau" no longer figures into my life. But the reality is that I still sin more than I want to admit and that I act like I belong to the dominion of darkness. My transformation is not yet complete.

The crux of the matter, however, is this: At the end of the day, if I do not see my sin as God sees it—and react to it as he reacts to it—then I am not equipped for spiritual warfare. Unless I understand that God hates *all* sin, I am in danger of playing spiritual games that deny the reality of my rebellion against our Creator and leave me open to attack from the tempter who would destroy me. Coming to terms with my sin is one of the essentials. Spiritual warfare is not just "out there" against demons and principalities but also "in here," the inner battle against the power of sin in my heart and mind.

Satan's "Handles"

Paul told the Ephesians that they should not leave anger to linger so that they would not "give the devil a foothold" (Eph. 4:27). Each time we sin and do not deal with it, a "handle" pops up in our lives by which Satan can grab hold and pull us down. This doesn't mean that every time we sin a demon comes to reside in us. Rather, it means that sin we do not confess before God holds us back in our Christian growth. Walking the Christian life is enough work in itself; imagine trying to do it with hundreds of handles for the enemies of God to pull on that slow or stop our progress!

Paul goes on to tell Christians to strip off and replace those things that are rotting because of sinful and deceptive desires:

➤ Put off false living; speak and live truthfully

➤ Put off festering anger; deal with anger through kindness, compassion, and forgiveness

➤ Put off mooching from others (this includes stealing from our employers); work honestly and faithfully

➤ Put off foul or slanderous talk; speak things that are helpful and encouraging

We take these "rags" off by recognizing them for what they are, repenting of them before God, and turning our back on them. We "put on" the new self by allowing the Holy Spirit to control and empower our lives (Eph. 5:18). By stripping off the old and putting on the new, we discipline ourselves in the Christian life, becoming stronger for spiritual warfare. But why is it so hard to follow this spiritual discipline? Because in order to unmask sin in our lives, we must come to terms with hidden things like pride, anger, and lust.

Pride is at the core.
Pride is the result of an inappropriate focus on self. It does not always take the form of vanity; pride can also be self-deprecating in a self-centered way. Take careful note of C. S. Lewis's remarks on pride in his classic *Mere Christianity:*

> There is one vice of which no man in the world is free; which everyone in the world loathes when he sees it in someone else; and of which hardly any people, except Christians, ever imagine that they are guilty.... There is no fault which makes a man more unpopular, and no fault which we are more unconscious of in ourselves. And the more we have it ourselves, the more we dislike it in others.[2]

For many, pride so infects us that we cannot separate ourselves from it. We grow up in an atmosphere of pride, which we breathe in all too deeply from cradle to grave. In *Changing on the Inside*, John White writes, "Curiously, pride is the very quality we try to inculcate into our children for their good. We define it, to be sure, as self-respect. . . . In other words we teach our children as we were taught ourselves—to overcome weaknesses and vices by pride."[3]

The book of Proverbs mentions pride many times. God hates pride (8:13); it brings disgrace (11:2); it breeds quarrels (13:10); it brings us low (29:23); and it leads to destruction (16:18). Ultimately, pride must even look down on God. Thus it is viewed as the core of sin and the heartbeat of evil. I dare not underestimate its role in my life when I come before God to confess my sins. In the New Testament, we are admonished to humble ourselves before God *before* we resist Satan (see James 4:7 and 1 Pet. 5:6-8).

Pride puts us in Satan's camp. To put it baldly, spiritual pride is a declaration of allegiance to Satan and his ways. It is idolatry of the deepest type, the most difficult to root out. By the exercise of pride we declare to God that we do not need him—it is no wonder that he removes his protection. In effect, he is simply responding to our own attitude by saying, "You say you don't need me? Fine, let's see how you do for a while without my blanket of protection over you."

Our goal in rooting out and exposing pride is not to fall for the idea that it will ever be fully conquered. Pride is always a possibility, and we must be alert to the ways it shows itself in our lives. Facing pride on a daily basis requires an attitude of humility rather than particular words to pray or claims of authority. Power encounters are not the central weapon against pride; disciplined vigilance is.

On the personal front, think about some of the ways that pride might be expressed in your life. Do you get too defensive over relatively minor things? When you make a mistake, do you stew or get angry over it, berating yourself or finding someone else to blame? Are you the constant subject of your conversations? Do you feel that you don't really need others to get along in life? All of these are indications of the work of pride. We must humble ourselves before God, asking him to extract that insidious root of pride that we all carry.

Anger drives us to hurt others.

I did not know how often I was angry until I got married. My wife would say, "Are you angry?" I would snarl back, "No!" Eventually I began to see that I was denying my anger, at least in part because it made me look better to myself. I admit that I didn't like what I saw. That is a reality of exposing sin—we won't like what God shows us.

All of us have experienced anger, and for many that anger lies unresolved under the surface. It leaks out by the way we handle the inconveniences of life. If a small inconvenience causes you to vent a stream of invectives, perhaps you need to ask God to begin to show you what anger is driving you and how that anger can be resolved. If you have long thought of yourself as one who simply has a short temper, then a time of introspective prayer, asking God to reveal possible reasons for that tiny fuse, will be helpful in cultivating the fruit of patience.

Do you know any bitter people? Often they have been hurt deeply and are angry on the inside. Having nowhere else to go, their anger leaks out as a constant venom, poisoning their relationships. The problem is that, in trying to tap the source of the bitterness, they must be ready to face the underlying anger—and that is a frightening thing! It is easier to keep it buried. But that is not how God deals with anger.

It should be said, though, that *anger is not always evil in and of itself.* How we deal with anger is more important than its presence. Jesus' anger boiled over at the moneychangers in the temple, and he destroyed their tables. His anger was righteous indignation. Ours, all too often, is that of self-righteous pettiness or displaced pain. We will return to this issue in the discussion on forgiveness, which is the key to dealing with anger.

Do you find yourself angry at small things? Do you boil over when something does not go your way? Do you find yourself simmering over events that happened long ago? Take the time before God to ask him to root out the sources of your anger, to help you see the way it drives and controls you, and to help you release its bitter poison from your system in constructive ways.

Lust entices us.
Lust is an unbridled appetite or desire. The desire itself may not be evil, but the way it controls us can be used by Satan as a source for evil. Lust can be found in appetites (food, sex) as well as desires (greed, covetousness). Food, sex, and material things are not evil in themselves. They are good things provided by God. However, when desired or used inappropriately, they are enticements to sin.

We often find ready excuses to fulfill our lusts, and we can be very creative and even self-righteous about it. "I deserve this," "No one will ever know," "A little bit won't hurt," "I really *need* this" are such frequent litanies that we don't even take the time to examine the premises on which they stand. As a small example, I used to look carefully over the full-color, pullout ads in our Sunday newspaper. It was amazing how often I could find things that I really "needed" just by looking at the pictures! Advertisers play on this regularly, as do producers in all areas of mass media. Pictures are not only worth a thousand words, they stimulate the senses and engage our emotions. God calls us to see our justifications for what they are, bring them before him as wrong, and turn our backs on them.

In what ways does lust drive you? Do you tell yourself how much you *need* something (whether sexual release, food, or material goods) in order to rationalize it? Ask God to begin the process of showing you how your lusts drive you, so that you can face them more honestly and battle the enemy in this area.

Unmasking Sin on Each Front

We've looked at God's view of our sin and how Satan uses our human weaknesses to pull us down. Now let's get more specific and consider some applications of unmasking sin on the other fronts of spiritual warfare.

On the up-close-and-personal front, come before your loving Creator to ask him to expose to you the ways you are driven by pride, anger, and lust. Ask him to reveal the hidden pockets in your life that hinder your growth in and fellowship with Christ. Let him lovingly and tenderly begin the process of bringing to the surface those attitudes of rebellion that lie underneath so that they can be brought to the cross and dealt with in a way that helps us grow in our spiritual pilgrimage.

The interpersonal front is where the exposure of sin can get far more sticky. For example, if you sense God's call to expose pride in another person, you had better be ready for a counter-attack that exposes the log in your own eye. The pilgrimage God calls us to is one of accountability. We are not to ignore sin but to encourage each other to do good works. The enemy delights in playing on our fears ("He'll kill me if I tell him that!") and cultural values ("That's her business, not mine.") to keep us from lovingly, gently, and humbly exposing sin in the lives of others.

This isn't a license to crusade and judge others. But we don't want to neglect the responsibility we have as brothers and sisters to hold each other accountable to godly living. Keeping these two possibilities in tension will help us discover Christ-honoring ways to unmask sin in each other and provide help to deal with what has been unmasked.

What is true on the interpersonal front is also true in our relationships in our local churches. At this level, the accuser delights as much when *no* sin is being uncovered as he does when witch-hunts are used to inappropriately accuse people. The result of the former is a cover-up leading to hypocrisy. The result of the latter is pain and alienation, which is destructive rather than restorative.

Keep in mind the goals of exposing sin: repentance and restoration. A general rule of thumb that most people follow is that exposure of sin should be only as public as the sin itself. The method Jesus outlined in Matthew 18:15-17 is to go to the offender privately and, if that does not work, to bring witnesses and, if that fails, to bring it before the congregation.

The universal church of Christ needs to battle sin on the systemic front by standing against the dehumanizing and alienating practices of the social institutions of the cultures in which we live. Exposure of sin on this front may be done through individual Christians and churches speaking up in the public arena. (At times this may even be against Christian institutions that, whether knowingly or unknowingly, have committed themselves to courses of sinful domination or behavior.) This could involve supporting causes through selective participation in demonstrations, boycotts, and even civil disobedience. It may be expressed through art or music. We may need to involve ourselves more in the political process by voting, by informing appropriate local and national representatives of our perspectives, or by even running for office when our voices are not being heard.

Uncovering sin on any level is never easy and is never an end in itself. It always has the goal of moving beyond the exposure to genuine and deep-seated change. In the next chapter we turn to the weapons of repentance and confession, which are essential in the spiritual battle of stripping off sin.

8

Putting Sin behind Us

As a young boy, I had a deep love for science-fiction stories. I thought I had died and gone to heaven when, in fourth grade, I discovered and read my first Tom Swift book. From the Tom Swift series to the books of such well-known science-fiction authors as Isaac Asimov and Arthur C. Clarke, I read away the hours, content in my world of advanced scientific inventions, futuristic scenarios, and outer-space adventures. Often there were summer days when I would do nothing but read. Run around out in the hot summer sun? Not for me! Just give me an air-conditioned room, a nice couch, a pile of books, and a large bag of chips, and I was set for the rest of the day.

I continued my voracious reading for pleasure throughout college, my first term of missionary service, and seminary. After graduation, I prepared to return to Kenya to teach and decided to give my book collection away. After all, as a professor, I needed to move on. After I arrived in Nairobi, however, I found several secondhand bookstores that stocked science fiction. I began to buy books again. A year after arriving in Kenya, I married. Six months into our marriage, I realized that my pleasure reading was more than a "habit." I did not control it; it controlled me. It also began getting in the way of my relationship with Emily. We would have a disagreement, and I would go and read for a few hours. I was entertained; Emily was alone.

It dawned on me that I faced a choice. I could make a break

with this dominating habit, or I could be overwhelmed by it. On a peaceful Sunday afternoon, I simply confessed to God that I realized I had been trying to serve two masters. I admitted to him that I had become enslaved to my reading and that I needed to break from it. I decided to turn my back on it, and I announced that I would no longer allow it to be used as a tool in my life. I collected my books, lit a small fire in our charcoal grill, and burned them. Now I am not advocating a general policy of burning books! But in my case, it was a symbol before God of my desire to break cleanly with the past. The habit was broken. My obsession with science-fiction books died in the confession and the fire.

The Power of Confession and Repentance

This may seem a rather trivial illustration of personal spiritual warfare. Yet I count it as one of the more significant events of my life. I came to grips with something that had been a part of me for more than twenty years, and with God's help, I turned my back on it. As far as I am concerned, *that is what spiritual warfare is all about.* It is not primarily about fighting spectacular cosmic battles in the heavenly places but about winning the very real (and, at times, very trivial) battles in the context of real life. As the more experienced demon Screwtape wrote to the neophyte Wormwood in *The Screwtape Letters:*

> You will say that these are very small sins; and doubtless, like all young tempters, you are anxious to be able to report spectacular wickedness. But do remember, the only thing that matters is the extent to which you separate the man from the Enemy. It does not matter how small the sins are, provided that their cumulative effect is to edge the man away from the Light and out into the Nothing. Murder is no better than cards if cards can do the trick. Indeed, the safest road to Hell is the

gradual one—the gentle slope, soft underfoot, without sudden turnings, without milestones, without signposts.[1]

Satan wants to keep us on that downward slope with everyday sins as well as more potent ones. We must make use of the weapons of confession and repentance in our fight against sin.

The first step in dealing with personal sin is to unmask it, then confess it before God and repent by turning from it. When we confess our sins, we are assured of God's forgiveness (1 John 1:8-9).

Confession does not have to be part of a special ritual. To *confess* simply means "to say the same thing as" God does about our sin. In other words, what God has called sin we also call sin. We admit our sins to God and then rest in the assurance of his promised forgiveness. When we honestly face up to the hate our sin has shown toward God and the hurt we have caused, then we can confess and accept the forgiveness extended to us by Christ. Our warfare responsibility is to regularly pray that God will uncover the things in our lives that are displeasing to him so that we can turn from them.

Once we have admitted our sin, repentance takes us a step further. In the Bible, the act of repentance is an extension of confessing. The word translated *repent* literally means "to turn around." Symbolically, it refers to turning our backs on sin—stopping the sinful activity—and walking in a new direction. This inevitably involves lifestyle changes and may require creative advance planning to avoid situations where a temptation is overwhelming to us.

"But often I don't *feel* repentant," you say. Or, "I can't win. I do the same things over and over." Remember we are in a war. It is a struggle and a process. But don't give up. Turning our backs on sin is always a cooperative effort between God and us. We have to want to stop, but God gives us the energy we need to carry out that desire. God the Father is with us, Christ has won the ultimate victory over the power of sin, and the Holy Spirit enables us to continue the fight.

Breaking Habitual Sin

On a deeper level, we can become overwhelmed by sin that has been practiced regularly until it has become an enslaving habit. My love of reading science-fiction books had become an addiction rather than just a habit. Until I could see that this habit was controlling me, however, I was not ready to discard it. God had to give me a new perspective. I had to see from the inside how insidious it was in my marriage before I was willing to label it for what it was: sin.

With the sin exposed, God worked in me so that I no longer wanted it to dominate my life. I not only recognized my activities as sin in my head, I *felt* them as sin in my heart. They became a crushing weight holding me down, and I desperately wanted change. Out of my brokenness, I committed my will by submitting myself to God's work in my life to bring about that change. He gave me the strength to turn my back on that habit and take action. Simple confession would not have been enough to break the back of my sin in this situation. It required an act that demonstrated my genuine acknowledgment of and turning from the sin. Through the miracle of repentance, the bonds of habitual sin were broken.

With this kind of sin, we need to find a meaningful way to make a break with its enslaving power. More often than not, this will involve bringing the habit into the light. This can be difficult. To admit to being enslaved by a sinful habit can be a humiliating experience. Many would prefer to lose the battle in silence rather than win it by confessing it to another Christian. This is especially true of sexual sins.

The bottom line, however, is that confession *by itself* is almost never enough to break habitual sins. We need to find one or more trusted friends who will hear us out and help us think through a means of breaking the habit. Sometimes this will involve a change of lifestyle or a recognition of the situations that typically lead to temptation and fall. For example, if pornography is a problem, it certainly is not wise to purchase cable service that provides access to pornographic movies. Neither is it wise to rent videos that depend on explicitly sexual themes. If the problem is impulse buying as a means of relieving frustration or guilt, it might be wise to tear up the credit cards and pay off the debts.

In some cases, it will be helpful to set up a "hot line" by which you can call a friend who will either pray with you or come over to be with you when you sense temptation coming on. Romans 12:21 tells us, "Don't be overcome by evil, but overcome evil with good." Be as creative in finding ways to break habits as you have been in perpetuating them.

Avoiding the Occult

In spiritual warfare, it is especially important to unmask the sin of occult involvement. God is very clear that his children are to have no involvement with the occult, even in fun. Before the people of Israel entered Canaan, they were told that they were to avoid any of the occult practices of the people then living in the land:

> When you enter the land the LORD your God is giving you, do not learn to imitate the detestable ways of the nations there. Let no one be found among you who sacrifices his son or daughter in the fire, who practices divination or sorcery, interprets omens, engages in witchcraft, or casts spells, or who is a medium or spiritualist or who consults the dead. Anyone who does these things is detestable to the LORD, and because of these detestable practices the LORD your God will drive out those nations before you. You must be blameless before the LORD your God. The nations you will dispossess listen to those who practice sor-

cery or divination. But as for you, the LORD your God has not
permitted you to do so. (Deut. 18:9-14)

The principle of the Christian avoiding the occult in all its forms
still applies today. This is especially important in a culture where
the occult has experienced a resurgence in popularity. From
Ouija boards to newspaper horoscopes to channeling to "dial-a-
psychic" services, we are bombarded with opportunities. Granted,
most of these are bogus and do not engage genuine satanic
power. At the same time, even engaging in bogus activities stands
as a defiant statement before God that we do not trust him to
meet our needs in life and to provide for us, giving a handle for
the enemy to use to slow our growth in Christ.

Admittedly, the occult can hold a certain fascination. Our
curiosity is piqued by special powers or the possibility of knowing the future. The occult's promise of knowledge, security,
significance, power, and success holds many people today in its
grip. As much as I might try to distinguish between parlor games
and genuine involvement, the Bible makes no such demarcation.
All occult activity is prohibited, for it leads us on a direct path to
Satan and his desire to dominate our lives.

If you are involved in the occult, confess and turn away from
it. If you have any objects that you have used for occult practices,
I recommend that you get rid of them. This is not because demons
are somehow attached to them but because the objects represent
your defiance of God's prohibition against the occult. By hanging
on to them, you are leaving a door open for further involvement.
Getting rid of these things demonstrates your commitment to
turn your back on them.

Dealing with Sin on Each Front

Throughout this chapter we have focused on putting sin behind us in our personal walk. The practice of confession and

repentance has vital implications for the other warfare fronts as well—in relationships with each other, in the local church, and within the larger world system.

Confess to each other.

For many of us, nothing could be more frightening or uncomfortable than to confess sins to another person, especially if the sins we confess are ones we still face. Yet in James 5:16, Christians are admonished to "confess your sins to each other and pray for each other so that you may be healed." Here James provides a link between confession and healing. While the meaning of healing in the context here is certainly physical, it also addresses a spiritual reality.

This each-other confession is not to be a one-time act. The verb tense in the original Scripture indicates a present, continuous action. James does not say that this confession is necessary for healing, though it is part of the healing process here. He does not say that we are to confess every sin, though that is certainly allowable the way the text is written. Also, he does not say that we are to confess the morbid details of each sin. The concept is that we admit the sin without weighing down the mind of our brother(s) or sister(s) in Christ with the full details. The attitude taken by the one hearing the confession is shown by Paul in Galatians 6:1-2: "Brothers, if someone is caught in a sin, you who are spiritual should restore him gently. But watch yourself, or you also may be tempted. Carry each other's burdens, and in this way you will fulfill the law of Christ."

Confessing our own sin is one thing. But how do we go about repenting and confessing to people whom we have sinned against? I think there are four critical overlapping steps in this process.

First, we must honestly face up to the hurt we have inflicted. We cannot deny it or denigrate it; we must empathetically see it from the side of the one we have hurt. At the very least, this will involve listening to their side of the story (if they are willing to tell it to us). We are not looking to justify our own actions, but to see them as wrong in God's sight.

Second, we admit the wrongdoing to God and accept the forgiveness that Christ offers. We recognize that our sin has become a barrier to our own fellowship with God. We do this with the hope that God will work to restore the human relationships we have broken.

Third, we go to the person who was offended and ask for forgiveness. This does not have to be done verbally; written apologies are more appropriate in some circumstances. At that time, they will have a responsibility before God to forgive us. The honesty and empathy they see in our confession will make that path easier for them to walk. Because of our sin against them, however, their trust in our ability to relate to them in a godly fashion has been broken.

Fourth, we must be willing to accept any appropriate boundaries set by the other party. We must allow time (and a clean track record) for trust to be rebuilt.

Deal with sin in the church.

All that we have said above concerning repentance and confession applies in the local church as well. Here we simply extend the circle of those who know the sin. It is no longer just God and a trusted friend who know about it; I share it also with an appropriate church leader, who will help restore me and carry the burden of my fallenness with me. Often this sets me free from the nagging worry of the skeleton in my closet. In addition, by seeing brothers and sisters in Christ able to hear my sin and still accept me, I get a glimpse on the human level of what God does on the divine level. We need to create an atmosphere in our churches in which brokenness, rather than the facade of perfection, is welcomed and encouraged.

The Corinthian church enjoyed a wonderful experience of

God's power. Miracles were overflowing. God's work was evident. At the same time, a certain man in the congregation was sleeping with his father's wife (1 Cor. 5:1-6). What did the church do? They justified it! The culture in which the church was located was known for its sexual freedom; they apparently felt this offense was not worth the bother.

Reports of this reached Paul, who had originally started the church. The hardest part for Paul was not just that this was taking place but that the church was even proud and boastful about it. His response was radical, even by today's standards. In sharp terms, he commanded the church to expel the man from their fellowship. He reminded them that they should be mourning their actions, not bragging about them.

Paul's desire was not punishment but discipline. He commanded that they "hand this man over to Satan." In other words, cast him out of the protective fold of the Christian community into the world, the sphere in which Satan operates. Paul's hope was that this extreme action would stop Satan's attempt to destroy this church through its toleration of this sin. He didn't want the man literally destroyed, but disciplined and restored to faith.

This seems harsh in our own time and culture. How often do we hear the dictum "Do not judge, lest you be judged"? While we are to tolerate certain things, this case shows us that there is a line that must not be crossed. If there is sin that infects the whole church and opens the door to contamination, it must be dealt with. We are not to use this to start a new Inquisition, but neither are we to shirk from the responsibility of honestly facing sin in our midst as local churches. We err by tolerating everything just as much as we err by tolerating nothing.

The Corinthians were not the only Christians in the New Testament who needed to repent as a community. Five of the seven churches Jesus addresses in Revelation 2–3 were also told to repent. The sins that they needed to turn away from included loss of their "first love" for God, listening to false teachers, tolerating false prophets, spiritual deadness, empty boasting, and pride. These were presented as sins of the whole church, for which the church as a whole must repent.

Corporate repentance, however, must be led by church leaders. Not everyone will have the same attitude toward the action being taken. Some will feel strongly that it must be done, others will wonder what all the fuss is about, and still others will feel that the church should avoid any public airing of "dirty laundry." Satan will try to exploit this environment. Great caution should be taken that the sins being put off are truly congregational sins and that the methods used for confession and repentance are culturally relevant and seek to honor Christ above all.

Challenge social evils in our culture.

It had to be one of the most frightening moments of the prophet Nathan's life. How would you feel if it was your task to tell the president of your company that he was living in sin? You might lose your job. Nathan stood to lose his life. King David had committed adultery with Bathsheba and then arranged her husband's murder in battle (2 Sam. 11:1–12:25). Nathan knew that God had called him to expose the king's sin in a public setting.

The method Nathan chose was indirect. He told a parable that led David to think a great wrong had been done by someone else in the kingdom. So David pronounced his judgment on the man. When Nathan told him that *he* was the man, David repented of his act.

This is one of countless examples in the Bible of God's people speaking out against social wrongs. The prophet Elijah confronted Israel's prophets for serving the false god Baal rather than the true God. Ezekiel served as a watchman of God's judgment against a culture steeped in sin. Amos denigrated the nation's leadership for oppressing the needy and pampering themselves. Jeremiah proclaimed God's truth in the teeth of violent and repressive opposition. Jonah reluctantly preached to Nineveh and witnessed the entire city repent.

Today the church faces issues that are tearing our culture apart, ranging from abortion to sexual orientation to genetic experiments to environmental problems. A church that is equipped for the challenge of spiritual warfare is one that is engaging the culture in dialogue and exposing the cultural system for what it is.

Do we expose the materialistic attitudes that pervade both the church and society? Do we expose the dependence on performance that dominates the Sunday morning pulpit just as much as it does the workplace? Do we expose the power grabbing that infects us at all levels of society, from committee meetings to boardrooms? These are hard questions, but we must be asking them if we are to live as kingdom citizens, shining light in a dark world. We must not lose sight of the real enemy. It is not just against flesh and blood that we struggle. When the church is sidelined, Satan will always win the battle for the mind of the culture.

Repent of sins for the culture.

When a people, culture, city, state, or country comes to the stage of repenting, how should that be expressed? Some spiritual warfare practitioners advocate a type of repentance in which an appropriate person, or group of people, repents on behalf of a people or nation. They call this *identificational repentance,* meaning that the person or group is identifying itself as an appropriate representative for the people or nation that has sinned.

There are a number of biblical instances of identificational repentance. For example, Nehemiah confessed the sins of Israel and his family before God, asking God to restore the exiles (Neh. 1:5-11). God responded, using Nehemiah himself as the leader to rebuild the walls of Jerusalem. In 2 Samuel 21, we are told that when Israel faced a three-year famine, God revealed to David that the famine was a judgment for the suffering of the Gibeonites at the hands of Saul. David mediated on behalf of Saul and Israel, demonstrating repentance and allowing the execution of seven of Saul's descendants by the Gibeonites. As a result, God once again answered prayers on behalf of the land. In both of these cases, the ones repenting were godly people who were both *political* and *spiritual* leaders.

In light of these examples, the key consideration is whether the person repenting can truly be said to be an *appropriate* representative of the will and hearts of the people. Recently, Japanese church leaders repented on behalf of Japan's atrocities during World War II to Korean church leaders, and great healing has taken place among those who took part in the meetings. Members of the Southern Baptist Convention repented of their ancestors' involvement with the slave trade, yielding reconciliation among some black and white churches. These events are powerful. At the same time, until these church leaders represent the will of the people as a whole, the spiritual dynamics of repentance from the sin will not be released into the larger culture. Identificational repentance is an area that is relatively new in mission circles. While it offers tremendous potential for restoration within church circles, it will not carry beyond the church unless the larger culture is involved.

Don't Just Read about It

In these last two chapters we have discussed the dark side of our lives and its relation to spiritual warfare. It is not enough just to *read* about the ways we need to confront sin; we must actually deal with it. If we are not convicted by God about the depths of our sin and do not in his power strip off the things that Satan can use to pull us down, we cannot expect to live lives full of the freedom Christ offers. This is the core of spiritual warfare.

Therefore, before moving on to the next chapter, I encourage you to put this book down and take the time to prayerfully consider what areas of sin in your life God might be inviting you to confess and turn your back on. Ask him to show you if there are people to whom you need to confess and repent for things you have done. Let him speak to you about any sin issues in your church that need to be taken care of before God will release his loving touch among you. Finally, sit quietly before him, asking if there are ways you can begin to address the sins of your culture that will unshackle the society around you from Satan's power.

9

Loving and Enjoying God

On my first day of college, one of my teachers announced that she was not a Christian. The reason? The idea of sitting on a cloud and playing a harp for all of eternity sounded more like hell than heaven to her. Her view of Christianity is a common one: boring. Christians are often thought of as party poopers who have no idea how to really enjoy life. And unfortunately, some Christians live out the stereotype.

The preacher Billy Sunday said, "If you have no joy in your religion, there's a leak in your Christianity somewhere." I am convinced that Satan is fiendishly satisfied when our relationship with God is a drudgery of rules and regulations. When he can squeeze the joy and delight out of our walk with Christ, he has succeeded in producing a dour Christian, who stands as a testimony for others to avoid. Yet Jesus said, "I have told you this so that my joy may be in you and that your joy may be complete" (John 15:11).

I have to confess that the idea that we are actually to enjoy and delight in God came as a shock the first time I encountered it. John Piper's refreshing book *Desiring God: Meditations of a Christian Hedonist* exposed my false ideas of relating to God. The term *Christian hedonist* struck me as an oxymoron. But Piper maintains that the best way to glorify God is to enjoy him. A Christian hedonist, then, is someone who seeks out pleasure *in God*. The issue is not happiness, which is dependent on circumstances. Rather, the issue is enjoying God for who he is and what he has given us.

Later, I cranked up my computer concordance and searched for the occurrence of words like *enjoy, joy, rejoice,* and *delight* in the book of Psalms. The printout was nine pages long, containing more than 140 verses! And this was just from one book of the Bible. There were countless things to delight in: protection (16:8-11), salvation (35:9), deliverance (97:10), and, of course, God himself (68:3-4). God gives us few greater gifts than the ability and pleasure in delighting in him, and he wants us to experience that delight to its fullest.

We have talked about putting off sin through confession and repentance. But it is nearly impossible to eliminate sinful practices unless we also develop an opposite and correspondingly positive lifestyle. If we take off old rags, we then have to *put on* new clothes. When we put on the Christian disciplines of Bible study and prayer, they will bring us into a more intimate relationship with our Creator. We are not just learning how to resist Satan, but we are learning *how to love God.*

Loving God through Bible Study

One way we love God is by coming to know him through the study of the Bible. By studying, memorizing, and meditating on Scripture, we will learn principles for living life as God designed it.

Study to gain wisdom for life.

Learning about God comes through Bible study focused on application. Strive to go beyond simply getting information into your head. As Tim Hansel wrote in *You Gotta Keep on Dancing,* "All of our theology must eventually become biography. The constant challenge in this life we call Christian is the translation of all we believe to be true into our day-to-day lifestyle."[1] Reflect on what you discover and be creative in finding ways to apply the truths you pick up. Keeping a journal of the things you are learning can be helpful.

The discipline of personal Bible study is to be a regular, ongoing, lifetime habit. As one who was trained in seminary, my biggest struggle with Bible study is the danger of doing it simply because I have to preach or teach from it, not because I want to know more about God, myself, and my enemy. I have found that involvement in small-group Bible study is the easiest way to maintain my habit. When I know I'll be meeting regularly with a group of people who are also accountable, it is easier to carve out the time to study.

Do not think of "study" as limited to your own personal work in the Scriptures. It also includes listening to Bible-centered messages and reading good books dealing with important biblical issues. Additionally, audiotapes of the Bible are available, and they make for good listening while commuting or chauffeuring the family. Your local Christian bookstore will probably stock more Bible studies, commentaries, and good books than you can read in a lifetime—take advantage of living in the information age!

Hide God's Word in your heart.

The psalmist wrote, "I have hidden your Word in my heart that I might not sin against you" (Ps. 119:11). If we are to defend ourselves when the enemy attacks, we must have some ammunition at hand. When Jesus was tempted by Satan, he was able to quote Scripture (each passage was from Deuteronomy) and spot Satan's misinterpretations. He had the Word hidden in his heart, available for instant use. When I am tempted by the lottery, I find it invaluable to claim the truth of Philippians 4:19: "And my God will meet all your needs according to his glorious riches in Christ Jesus." In stating that truth, I am reminded to keep my focus on God as the one who meets my needs, not the lottery jackpot.

You might be saying, "Memorization is good, but I have never been able to do it." The ability to memorize is a human ability we all share. It amazes me when someone tells me he or she can't memorize the Bible, but then they rattle off sports statistics! Think of the meaningless songs and commercial jingles you have memorized without even trying. Perhaps you can start the process of memorizing simply by listening to some of the many Christian artists who have set Scripture to music. Another helpful method is to listen to Bible tapes. For those ready to dive in, a list of selected verses relevant to spiritual warfare is provided in appendix A. You may want to look them over and start with those that are most meaningful to your current situation. Verses that have an immediate application in our lives are easier to memorize.

Let God's Word sink deep.
Last, and possibly of greatest significance in our all-too-hurried culture, we are to carefully reflect and meditate on Scripture. John White provides a helpful definition of meditation:

> Meditation is the deliberate, disciplined practice of focusing our attention on a truth or an aspect of reality—ideally, on the truth of the loving presence of Christ in and with us. . . . Meditation means reflecting on truth, letting it sink in. Meditation involves silent musing . . . taking time daily to sit and ponder what is real.[2]

Meditation for the Christian is not a meaningless emptying of the mind. It is focused on filling the mind with God's truths, allowing them to percolate within us so that they become part of our "mental programming."

According to social scientists, our culture provides us with a type of mental software. In computers, software is the set of instructions that tell the computer what to do. Even though we are free to make choices of our own volition, we still operate on a set of basic software instructions that guide how we respond to the events in life. That software is developed as we grow, shaped by family experiences, cultural surroundings, and the choices we make in responding to their influences. Meditation on biblical truths gives us the opportunity to modify our "programming" so we respond in a godly way to life's events.

Do you ever replay conversations in your mind, imagining what you really should have said? One type of biblical meditation is to replay those conversations and imagine what Jesus might have done or said if he were in your place. How would he return a blessing for a curse? It is impossible for us to even guess the answer unless we have taken the time to learn his commands and memorize portions of his Word. By applying what we know to the situations we have faced, we are better prepared for future spiritual encounters.

Loving God through Prayer

"Every chain that spirits wear / Crumbles in the breath of prayer," wrote John Greenleaf Whittier. A story in the book of Mark confirms the importance and power of prayer in spiritual warfare. At one point, Jesus' disciples were unable to cast a demon out of an epileptic boy. After Jesus released the boy from bondage, the disciples asked him why they had been unsuccessful. Jesus replied, "This kind can come out only by prayer" (Mark 9:29).

Jesus possibly was indicating that this certain class of demons required a special emphasis on prayer for expulsion. Perhaps the disciples had begun to take their authority over demons for granted. Perhaps they had forgotten that it is God's power that overcomes demons and had begun to trust in themselves. Jesus does not give a specific prayer to use. It is not a specific prayer that seems to be the issue, but the attitude in prayer. This situation required prayer that showed *humble reliance on God as Deliverer,* not just prayer *against the demon.*

The goal of "putting on" prayer is to maintain an atmosphere of prayer in our lives. This is the only way we can obey Paul's command to pray without ceasing (1 Thess. 5:17). When he told the Ephesians to put on the armor of God in order to stand against Satan, he explained that they were to do it in a manner that was permeated by prayer in the Spirit (Eph. 6:18). The idea is to cultivate a continuous, two-way communication with God over all of the events, big or small, of life. For example, I found my daily commute much easier when I started praying for the driver who had just cut me off or the person I felt was driving too slow. My attitude toward other drivers began to change. I saw them as people, not just "that maniac behind the wheel." It also improved my own driving because I could relax more.

We all struggle with distractions and weariness in our prayer lives. But we are not left alone to do the work of prayer. Paul also discusses praying "in the Spirit." This involves being filled with the Spirit and also means that we pray as the Spirit prompts us. God's Spirit helps us to pray (Rom. 8:26-27). He connects our needs with our expression and brings them before God's throne.

No advice has helped my prayer life more than Neil Anderson's discussion on dealing with distractions in *Walking through the Darkness.* His counsel: Don't fight distractions; use them as opportunities for prayer. Maybe you suddenly remember the last detail of a presentation you will make today. Fine. Jot it down. But, more importantly, pray about the presentation and for the people who will be there. Perhaps your distractions are about your children. Turn those into prayers about the problems or issues your family is facing. Think of creative ways you can turn your concerns into conversation with your loving Father. Cultivating the practice of prayer is essential if we hope to successfully win the battle for our minds and truly enjoy and delight in God.

Loving God through Submission

To say that we develop love for someone through submitting to them can sound abusive today. Yet the Bible is very clear: we are to submit to God. Far from being abusive, he *is* the one who created us, who knows what is best for us, and who cares for us more than any other. He takes great delight in providing for our needs and wants us to live rich lives full of the greatest blessing he offers: intimacy with him.

Because we are made in his image and have been empowered by the Holy Spirit, we can choose whether or not we want to submit to him. This is critical to spiritual warfare. Before we can resist Satan, we are to submit to God (James 4:7). We grow in our ability to submit to him as we apply what we learn from the study of his Word. It is important to distinguish between wanting to submit and actually submitting. I may *want* to lose weight, but I may still *choose* to live on French fries and ice cream. Real submission, then, is making active choices to live as God intends us to live, and it always involves a crisis of our will.

My roommate in college was not a Christian, and he often said he did not want God telling him what to do. It seems deeply ingrained in American culture (and perhaps in fallen human nature) that when someone tells us what to do, we want to do the opposite. Many people have the idea that God is a tyrant, a dictator, or some kind of megalomaniac who gets a kick out of ordering us around. They are especially fearful that he takes a perverse delight in telling us to do something we don't want to do.

I vividly remember my own struggle in this area. I had been a Christian for only a few months when it suddenly dawned on me that God might have something in store for me other than being a research scientist or an engineer. The idea of being some sort of a minister scared me to death! I asked my friends about it and wrestled with the idea for several weeks. One of the leaders of the Christian ministry that I was involved with finally communicated to me that God could use me in *any* occupation. Greatly relieved, and having a clearer picture that God really did love me and was not waiting to ambush me with marching orders, I began to enjoy growing closer to Christ.

Almost two years later, God did call me into full-time Christian work. Before that happened, however, my heart softened. I changed from being absolutely set on a science career to being open to professional ministry while still pursuing what I enjoyed doing. It was not until my heart had changed that I sensed God's call. Thus began the adventure I still walk today—a path I would not have chosen for myself, but one that has offered me greater fulfillment than my own dreams would have ever realized.

Essentially what I faced was a crisis of my will. I was being asked to submit to God without knowing in advance what that might entail. I was given no guarantee except for the merciful love of One who knew me better than I knew myself. The biblical word for *submit* involves the surrendering of our will under the will of others (Phil. 2:3-4). Our culture, however, tells us that only wimps submit. Even some Christians think submission is a dirty word. Often the problem comes from past experiences of cowering under abusive human authority, especially when those people justify their evil, domineering habits with their claim to be God's representatives. But submission to God involves surrendering our will to him and trusting that he knows what is best for us. Submission to spouses or human leaders who are abusive is another thing altogether.

Loving God through Thank-You Therapy

Following Jesus' death and resurrection, the disciples experienced miracles and conversions as they preached the gospel—events that led to their arrest by the religious leaders. According to Acts 5, they were brought before the leaders and whipped, before being released with a stern warning. But the disciples did not leave that place downcast or bitter. No, they left "rejoicing because they had been counted worthy of suffering disgrace for the Name" (Acts 5:41). Rejoicing? Rejoicing! They had learned the secret of a contentment independent of circumstances, a truth Paul wrote about while he too was unjustly jailed many years later (Phil. 4:12). They took the intended punishment and turned it upside down, just as their lives had been turned upside down by their relationship with Jesus. They were obeying the command Jesus gave in the Sermon on the Mount: "Blessed are you when people insult you, persecute you and falsely say all kinds of evil against you because of me. Rejoice and be glad, because great is your reward in heaven, for in the same way they persecuted the prophets who were before you" (Matt. 5:11-12).

The disciples' reaction to their suffering provides a challenge for us today. We are to nurture a personal habit of trusting and thanking God in all of life's circumstances. James tells us to consider it pure joy when we face trials (James 1:2). Peter tells his readers, who were facing persecution, to rejoice that they "participate in the sufferings of Christ" (1 Pet. 4:13). We are to learn how to see the bad things that happen through the lens of God's continuing sovereignty.

Paul commands us to give thanks in everything (1 Thess. 5:16-18; Col. 4:2). His command is not that of a naive and pampered man who lived a life of leisure. Read some of what he endured:

Five times I received from the Jews the forty lashes minus one. Three times I was beaten with rods, once I was stoned, three times I was shipwrecked, I spent a night and a day in the open sea, I have been constantly on the move. I have been in danger from rivers, in danger from bandits, in danger from my own countrymen, in danger from Gentiles; in danger in the city, in danger in the country, in danger at sea; and in danger from false brothers. I have labored and toiled and have often gone without sleep; I have known hunger and thirst and have often gone without food; I have been cold and naked. (2 Cor. 4:24-27)

How can we be thankful in the midst of our circumstances? Thankfulness is one of the results of being filled with the Spirit and letting Christ's peace rule in our hearts (Eph. 5:18-21; Col. 3:15-17). Thankfulness comes from choosing to let Christ do what he wants in us by his strength (Phil. 4:13). Too many people are waiting for circumstances to be right before they choose joy. They do not express their thanks to God until things are as they want them. We must "put on" the discipline of a thankful heart. One pastor I know calls this "thank-you therapy." What a wonderful expression! The term itself displays a godly attitude toward the discipline of giving thanks to God in all of the circumstances of life.

Loving God on the Wider Fronts

Moving from the personal arena of spiritual warfare, how can we grow in our love and enjoyment of God on the relational, corporate, and cultural fronts?

Every Christian should be part of a small group of like-minded believers who are striving to delight in God together through learning his Word and praying together. Help each other find new ways to submit to God through obeying what you are learning in his Word. Be sensitive to the Spirit's work in helping you learn how to thank God in all events of life. Celebrate God's love and provision.

Church leaders can model ways of learning to love and enjoy God. A wonderful example of helping the local church delight in God is the recent development in many churches of the use of choruses in worship and praise. The teaching of God's Word is also a part of spiritual warfare in the local church. Another exciting development is a growing awareness of the need to emphasize prayer, not just as a theological reality, but as a practice in the life of the church.

On the cultural front, our goal is to live as light in a darkened world. One of the realities of most of Western society is that it is slipping further and further away from our Judeo-Christian heritage. Many are even calling our culture *post*-Christian. Finding ways to be as wise as serpents but as innocent as doves in getting the world to interact with the truths of Christianity remains one of the greatest challenges of spiritual warfare in the West today. We need to ask God to show us the ways our culture is hurting and how the church can step in the gap to meet real needs that people have.

Basking in God's love is essential to your spiritual health. Before reading the next chapter, take stock of your own life. How can you learn to enjoy God and delight in him more? What can you do now to begin the process of studying his Word, memorizing small portions of it, and meditating on them throughout your day? Is there pain in your life that makes you frightened of submitting to God? Are there events in which you have not yet learned to thank God? Take some time to be with your Father, who wants you to delight in his love for you.

10

Loving and Enjoying People

Maybe you've had a Tim in your life. For me, Tim was one of those surprises God brings across our paths that change us forever. When I was in high school, I liked to think of myself as one of the "in" crowd. We thought we were good at studies, good at sports, good at life—at least good at *looking* like we had it all together.

Many of my friends had become Christians out of the same youth ministry in our high school, and we hung out together a lot. Tim, who had also come to Christ, began joining our activities—whether playing street hockey or our variations on baseball, football, or basketball. At the time, I hadn't really made any Christian commitment, preferring to watch and wait. One thing I was sure about, however; I knew that I did not like Tim. To my shame, I even took steps to make sure he was left out whenever possible.

During my senior year, things changed. First, over the Christmas break I finally decided to follow Christ. Second, my relationship with Tim changed.

Early that spring, our youth group announced a trip to Florida during spring break. Everyone was enthusiastic about going, but trips like that cost money. Two weeks before we were to leave, I found out that only two people had signed up and paid: Tim and I. So for the 168 hours of that spring break, Tim and I probably spent 167 of them together!

God used that trip to turn my cold-hearted attitude toward Tim into genuine love for him. Near the end of the week, I followed the prompting of God to confess to Tim what had been going on in me. I told him that if I had been honest with him earlier, I would have said that I hated him. The only reason I was able to admit it now was because God had turned my hatred upside down. Tim had to deal with *really* seeing me for the first time. I repented, and Tim forgave me.

From that time on we were inseparable. Sure, he still grated on my nerves. His habit of breaking out into a tone-deaf hymn while walking through the mall embarrassed me, and his corny jokes weren't any funnier than they were before. At the same time, Tim left an impact on me that lingers today. Sadly, Tim died in a car accident almost two decades ago, just before he graduated from college. His infectious love for Jesus ignited me with a flame that still burns. His willingness to forgive me taught me how to forgive others.

I noted earlier that Satan is a liar and a murderer, and that Adam and Eve's relationship was broken (or "murdered") by Satan's work in the Garden of Eden. Satan continues today to "murder" relationships whenever he can, and I've experienced that firsthand recently. I reluctantly pointed out to a woman who claims to follow Christ that she had cheated several friends of mine and was lying about what she had done. Her response was instant anger that I dared to call her a liar, and she immediately demanded an apology. I refused to back down, and together we drove the relationship past the breaking point. I am now faced with the results of a broken relationship. How can we keep and develop relationships with people while still holding them accountable for their character? How can we love people whether or not they ever respond to the truth?

My friend Tim was one of the few people to constantly challenge my faith and urge me to grow in my walk with Christ. He demonstrated what it meant to be a brother in Christ. This is an essential part of the spiritual armor we must wear when taking on the enemy. We must learn the art of loving each other in ways that will foster growth in Christlikeness. Just as we grow in our love and enjoyment of God, so we are to grow in our love and enjoyment of people who are made in God's image through humility, forgiveness, encouragement, and harmony through reconciliation.

The "One Another" Skills

In the book of Ephesians, Paul lays out some essential facts for the Christian pilgrim to know. He then applies that truth to a variety of real-life settings, ranging from slavery to family. The theme is simple: "Live a life worthy of the calling you have received" (Eph. 4:1).

We as a Christian community are to live and breathe the "each other" and "one another" commands sprinkled throughout the New Testament. These commands are built on the common theme of loving each other. The New Testament writers are not talking about feelings, but about behavior in life's circumstances. The commands about our commitment toward each other can be organized into four basic actions and attitudes: practicing humility, forgiving, encouraging one another, and living in harmony.

How do we put on the practices, actions, and attitudes that characterize loving one another? In Romans 12:2, Paul says that we must be transformed. He does not say that we must transform ourselves. Rather, we are to cooperate with God's transforming work in our lives through the ministry of the Spirit by seeking it and not hindering it. In his letter to the Philippians, Paul writes, "Therefore, my dear friends, as you have always obeyed, . . . continue to work out your salvation with fear and trembling, for it is God who works in you to will and to act according to his good purpose" (Phil. 2:12-13).

Practicing Humility

When I was a seminary student and still single, a young woman asked me if I knew what other women at our school thought of me. My curiosity was piqued, to say the least! She told me that they all thought that I was conceited, though she herself knew better. I was devastated. Was it true? Is that how people really saw me? Did I think too much of myself? Is that how I came across? To say it caused some deep soul-searching is an understatement. It launched a process that continues even today.

Paul suggests ways that Christians can avoid self-centered thinking. One way is to turn the focus from ourselves and be devoted to and honor one another (Rom. 12:10). We are to "put off" conforming to the world which demands that self be first, and "put on" an attitude that recognizes others' needs above our own. Similarly, Paul encouraged the Ephesians to be kind and compassionate to each other (Eph. 4:32), and he reminded the Galatians to serve one another (Gal. 5:13). We will not be able to serve one another if we are always thinking of ourselves first.

In my case, my friend's brutal honesty was a gift to me—not a pretty gift, to be sure, but a necessary one for my development as a Christian. I had to learn how to accept the truth and to seek God's power to be humble as he desires. Like me, you may still have a long way to go in "putting on" humble service for others. We all are in the process of trying to learn and live out Paul's attitude expressed in his letter to the Philippians:

> If you have any encouragement from being united with Christ, if any comfort from his love, if any fellowship with the Spirit, if any tenderness and compassion, then make my joy complete by being like-minded, having the same love, being one in spirit and purpose. Do nothing out of selfish ambition or vain conceit, but in humility consider others better than yourselves.

Each of you should look not only to your own interests, but also to the interests of others. (Phil. 2:1-4)

If we are to develop intimacy with each other, then we must humble ourselves. This can be taken to an extreme, however, in which abuse is enabled through a false understanding of being humble. Many think that to be humble they must have the lowest opinion of themselves that they can have. The truth, however, is that to be humble is simply to think of myself as God thinks of me, no more and no less. When I am able to think of myself as God thinks of me, then I will value being made in his image. I will respect my dignity as a person, and I will respect the dignity of other people. I will refuse to submit to abusive behavior but will not resort to the behavior of the abuser in the process. It is on this foundation that the ability to develop deep and genuine intimacy in relationships stands.

The Freedom of Forgiveness

Sam had grown up in what appeared to be an ideal American family. He felt comfortable and secure. That changed, however, when Sam found out a secret already known by everyone else in the family. For over a decade, Sam's mother had been having an affair with a close family friend. Sam did not learn of the affair until the girl he was dating, who happened to be the daughter of the man his mother was involved with, casually mentioned it.

Sam's innocent trust was broken, and he turned bitter—especially toward his mother, who had held a position of responsibility in the church while the affair was going on. What Sam needed was to be able to deal with the reality of living in a world in which those who are closest to you are the very ones who can hurt you the most through betrayal. In a word, Sam needed to learn how to forgive.

How can we tell Sam that he needs to forgive his mother for

her betrayal? How can we tell the victims of sexual abuse that their freedom in Christ comes in part by learning how to forgive those who have abused them? How can we require a grieving father to forgive his daughter's murderer? These difficult questions take us to a core issue in developing intimacy with people. Simply put, *if we cannot forgive, we cannot experience the freedom Christ offers.*

Jesus teaches that we are not ready to receive forgiveness for our sins unless we have forgiven others (Matt. 6:14-15). We will have great difficulty forgiving others if we do not understand how much we ourselves have been forgiven (Matt. 18:21-35). An unforgiving attitude may hold more people in spiritual bondage than any other problem.

Why is forgiveness so critical? Forgiveness is at the core of Christ's work on the cross: Because of his death, we have been fully forgiven. In telling us to take up our cross (Matt. 10:38), Jesus is telling us to follow him by doing the type of work he accomplished on the cross, namely, extending forgiveness to those who have sinned against us.

Extending forgiveness short-circuits several areas of Satan's attacks. When I forgive *myself,* I recognize my identity as a child of God who does not have to wallow in self-pity (all too often disguised as self-hatred). When I forgive *others,* they no longer have emotional holds on me, holds that disrupt the process of my maturing as a Christian. I am also relieved of the guilt that comes from refusing to forgive and freed to live righteously in relation to those who have hurt me.

The Forgiveness Myths

For some, forgiveness is associated with letting someone get away with something. For others, it means trying to forget the wrong done to you. As a result of my own struggles in this area, I have discovered that much of what I believed about forgiveness simply is not true. There are many lies and distortions about forgiveness in our churches. Have you accepted some of the following myths as truth?

Myth 1: I cannot forgive because . . . Many are trapped in the lie that they are unable to forgive. They come up with all types of excuses: it is too hard; so-and-so doesn't deserve to be forgiven; I deserved what happened; they couldn't help it; and so on. If anyone had the right to claim that he could not extend the offer to forgive, that person was Jesus. However, Jesus obediently walked the path God set before him, even forgiving those who carried out Satan's scheme to murder him. The truth is that God extended forgiveness to me through Christ, and he enables me to extend forgiveness to others as a response to his work in my life.

Myth 2: If I still remember, then I have not really forgiven. Some people think that the Bible teaches that God literally forgets the sins he forgives. God would no longer be omniscient if that were true. Rather, God's "forgetting" is a metaphor that shows us he no longer holds us to account for the sins he has forgiven. Genuine forgiveness involves living with the consequences of the action(s) of another, whether we remember them or not. To forgive, we remember all of the debt that was incurred, all of the pain we felt. We then choose to forgive the ones who hurt us and trust God to give us the power to wish them well. The familiar adage "Forgive and forget" would be better stated "Forgive and let go."

Myth 3: Time will eventually heal the pain even if I don't forgive. Anyone who has held on to a hurt for a long time knows that there is *some* easing of the pain as the event itself grows more distant. But while we may feel that time has healed the pain of the hurt, we often carry a desire for revenge that shows full healing has not taken place. In reality, time does not heal the deepest wounds; it just buries them. The only way to heal them is through processing what has happened and forgiving the one who hurt us.

Myth 4: Understanding the "why" behind the hurtful actions is the same as forgiving them. Understanding is an integral part of forgiveness. Even when we understand, we may not let go of our desire for revenge. There are times when understanding helps to significantly lessen the pain and gives one more freedom to forgive. However, explaining or excusing sin does not change that sin into something good; it simply explains the process that led to the sin. There is also the danger that when I explain away the evil that was done to me, I do so simply because it "costs" less to explain it than it does to recognize it as evil, confront it if necessary, and forgive.

Myth 5: Forgiving makes you a doormat for people to wipe their feet on. It may feel that in forgiving others we are simply opening up ourselves for further pain. This doormat myth may result from thinking that forgiveness eliminates the need for appropriate boundaries for others' actions. Forgiving someone does *not* mean that we can no longer hold them accountable for their actions; it simply means that we release them from our desire for personal revenge. The goal is to win a sister or brother, not to exact vengeance for our own hurt. Our forgiveness does not free others from facing the consequences that either society or God has for them. In forgiving others, we leave them in God's capable hands.

Myth 6: I don't need to forgive someone if they don't ask me or if they don't want it. This is the most debated area in dealing with personal forgiveness. Here are several responses.[1] Most important, my forgiving without the offender repenting of the misdeed is not the same as God's forgiving without repentance. For God to forgive without repentance would violate his justice. For me to forgive without repentance simply places the burden of justice for the wrong done squarely where it belongs—in God's hands.

Thinking that I can only forgive once the offender has repented may be a result of confusing reconciling with forgiving. To reconcile takes two; to forgive and offer a fresh start takes only one. In that sense, forgiveness is not the same as restoring the relationship. Rather, it moves us toward restoration.

We may distinguish between the offer of forgiveness and the acceptance of it. This is surely at the heart of Jesus' teaching about loving our enemies and Paul's telling us to overcome evil with good (Rom. 12:21). If we see forgiveness as a kingdom weapon to battle Satan's schemes to destroy relationships, then to withhold forgiveness from one who desperately needs it would be to play right into Satan's hands.

Because this is such a crucial part of loving each other and of spiritual warfare, I am including the following suggestions to help you in the process of forgiveness.

Do I need to forgive someone?

Here are some questions to consider that may shed light on your need to still forgive someone.[2] Reflect on them prayerfully.

1. Does the pain continue to control me? Does it continue to shape or even define my life? Is it leaking out in angry outbursts toward those I care about? Am I withdrawn from others because of fear of the pain that closeness may bring?

2. Am I looking for ways to get even and repay the pain I have felt? Do I withhold my approval? Do I withdraw when the offenders are present? Do I ignore or turn my back on their needs? Do I do everything to let them know how they have hurt me? Do I harbor a desire to destroy them and what they are trying to do in life? Do I gossip about them as a means of paying them back?

3. Can I wish them well—and even rejoice when good things happen to them? How do I feel when the ones who hurt me get a promotion, raise, or award? How do I respond when others praise them? Do I daydream of ways to get even? Am I able to pray for them, asking God to bless them?

How do I go about forgiving?

Earlier I mentioned Sam, whose mother's betrayal hit him deep in the heart. As we talked more, he shared how he hated his mom's adultery and hated his family for the lie they had lived over the past decade. While his mother was having an affair, everyone in the family was simply pretending that nothing was going on. At church, Sam felt like a hypocrite. At home, he simply felt miserable.

After explaining some of the process of forgiveness to him, he expressed his pain and anger, and then his choice to forgive his mother. He walked through each offense that he remembered, honestly and openly confessing the confusion, the hurt, and the hatred, and then releasing it to God. Drained but peaceful, he left.

Several weeks later I saw Sam again. Instead of a dour face, he was lit up with life inside. His home circumstances had not changed, but his attitude about them had. They no longer controlled him; the love of Christ did. He still had ups and downs, and there was buried pain to deal with, but the battle for him to live life as a child of the King of kings was won. He had peace in himself and was beginning to think through how reconciliation might be accomplished within the family. He was no longer driven by despair, but by hope. He now had a means of dealing with the pain that did not simply deny it or bottle it up for storage.

Forgiving begins when you choose to follow God's path whatever the cost. The process may be as simple as a declaration to God of your choice to forgive. Or it may take months (or years) to uncover the extent of your pain. Without actually launching the process, however, you can be sure you'll never complete it.

Start by asking God to show you anyone you need to forgive. As you consider the questions above, make a list of names. With the list in hand, announce your choice to forgive by simply stating the following sentence aloud: "I choose to forgive _____ for _____. I accept the pain that comes with releasing them from their debt to me."[3] As God brings events to mind, choose to forgive each one. Stick with a person until nothing more comes to mind, and then move on to the next name.

Dealing with deeper issues.
In many cases, the launching exercise deals with the problem, and nothing more needs to be done. There are also times when it is only the beginning of the work that needs to be done before complete healing takes place. This is generally true for cases of deep pain caused by either severe trauma or repeated abuse offenses over a long period of time. In these cases, a more extensive process is helpful and may require professional assistance. Figure 4 (see next page) illustrates the long-term process of coming to terms with painful events in our lives. Taking these steps toward forgiveness, and not being afraid to repeat steps when needed, will take us toward healing.[4]

The Power of Encouragement

Recently I preached at a church in Chicago as part of their missions conference. Afterwards I received a letter from the church expressing appreciation for my time among them. Even though my message had not been evangelistic, one person had responded by reconsidering his relationship with Christ. What fun it was for me to be told about it! The letter of thanks was an unexpected encouragement in my day. It picked me up, helped me realize that my time in preparation was worth it, and made me feel usable to God.

Satan wants to discourage us, but God tells us to encourage each other as an antidote to Satan's attacks. Hebrews 3:13 says, "But encourage one another daily, as long as it is called Today, so that none of you may be hardened by sin's deceitfulness." Paul writes, "Therefore, encourage one another and build each other up, just as in fact you are doing" (1 Thess. 5:11). He hoped to visit the Christians living in Rome because they would be able to encourage each other (Rom. 1:12). Apollos wanted to travel to Achaia, and the encouragement of the believers enabled him to go and minister powerfully there (Acts 18:27). Built up by

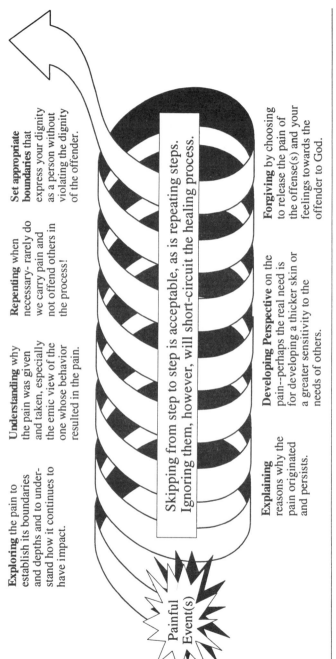

Exploring the pain to establish its boundaries and depths and to understand how it continues to have impact.

Understanding why the pain was given and taken, especially the emic view of the one whose behavior resulted in the pain.

Repenting when necessary- rarely do we carry pain and not offend others in the process!

Set appropriate boundaries that express your dignity as a person without violating the dignity of the offender.

Skipping from step to step is acceptable, as is repeating steps. Ignoring them, however, will short-circuit the healing process.

Explaining reasons why the pain originated and persists.

Developing Perspective on the pain--perhaps the real need is for developing a thicker skin or a greater sensitivity to the needs of others.

Forgiving by choosing to release the pain of the offense(s) and your feelings towards the offender to God.

Painful Event(s)

Figure 4
Steps toward Forgiveness of Deeper Pain

encouraging words from others, we can stand strong against the enemy's accusations. When we are encouraged, we are able to reframe our perspective on Satan's attacks and gain new energy to do what God is calling us to do.

I wonder how many Christians flag in their faith only because they have no one to encourage them. How many suffer in their own silent pain, disconnected from others who can lift them up when they are down? How many, buffeted by Satan, simply give up? This is an area where Christians can truly benefit from one another, giving each other the strength needed to keep their hearts and minds firmly focused on God, to the consternation of the enemy.

Take some time to ask God whom you might encourage. Is there a letter you need to write or a phone call you need to make? Do you need to support and uplift someone close to you: your spouse, child, parent, or family friend? Find some way to take the offensive in overpowering evil with good today.

The Beauty of Harmony

"How good and pleasant it is when brothers [and sisters] live together in unity!" the psalmist reminds us. This can be easier said than done. Is there more relational discord than harmony in your home or church? Paul commands us to live harmoniously, saying that we should humbly associate with anyone and not be proud of our position (Rom. 12:16). Peter expresses the same idea when he writes that we should live in harmony with one another by being compassionate and humble (1 Pet. 3:8). In spiritual warfare, maintaining harmony with others is critical. Satan's goal as a destroyer is to disrupt relationships, and Christians are much easier to attack when we are isolated and disjointed.

As I was working on this book, a student came into my office. A week earlier, I had met her in the hallway and jokingly asked if she had been avoiding me. I wasn't serious; I simply hadn't seen her for a while and was teasing her. When she came into my office, however, she confessed that she *had* been avoiding me. She had an unfulfilled obligation in a project we had worked on together, and she felt guilt every time she saw me. After a week of stewing, she came to apologize to me for not meeting her obligation and to confess her avoidance. The obligation was trivial to me, but she apologized and I accepted. In a minor way, this is the process of reconciliation, which *Webster's* defines as "the process of restoring friendship or harmony."

The key to maintaining harmony is the ability to reconcile our differences. Reconciliation requires a blending together of forgiveness and repentance. Both parties must be willing to work together. Paul exhorted the Christians living in Rome: "If it is possible, as far as it depends on you, live at peace with everyone" (Rom. 12:18). He recognized, too, that it was *not* always possible, in part because we have no control over others' reactions.

If you are ready to begin the process of reconciling with someone who has hurt you, I strongly advise that you have a trusted friend help you think through the following questions.

1. Is the other person ready to reconcile? There are people who are so locked into lifestyles of bitterness, pain, and revenge that the idea of confessing, forgiving, and reconciling is the most frightening thing they can imagine. Others enjoy inflicting pain on people, and they will be happy to manipulate the situation if it keeps you under their control. (In this case, reconciliation is not possible until the person has repented before God.)

2. Why do you want reconciliation? In one sense, it is a matter of obedience. In another sense—and this is true especially when we are estranged from people who are significant to us—we may feel that God somehow does not accept us if that person does not. Are you just looking for their approval? Are you looking for brokenness and contrition as a type of payback for the pain you have endured? Will seeing them on their knees before you make you feel better?

3. Can you accept the worst possible response? More often
than not, offenders deny ever doing anything wrong: "You're too
sensitive," "You misunderstood what I meant," "I didn't do it."
How will you handle that type of response? Do you have the
strength to face a blatant lie without losing your temper?

Reconciliation is the result of a mutual process of forgiving
and repenting. Offended and offender often both need to repent
and to forgive for reconciliation to be effected. The offender should
focus on what he or she should do to encourage the re-establishment
of the relationship, and the offended must be willing to hold the
offender accountable for the changes that are negotiated.

The Goal: Harmony on All Fronts

Our goal in "putting on" harmony in the local church is to build
up a community. A community is not just a collection of individuals—it takes on a life of its own determined by its history, by the
ways people respond to that history and build a future, and by the
community's dependence on God to grow and sustain it. An
essential element in our spiritual warfare is to be part of a community in which the needs of all are met, encouragement is given and
received, trust is developed and shared, and love is experienced.

This is important because a godly community provides a
buffer against the attacks of the enemy. It gives us additional
resources to draw on when we are overwhelmed. Finally, it
serves as a foretaste and preparation for our life in heaven—a
fact that helps keep the earthly battle in proper perspective. As
a community living in harmony, we are called to refuse to submit
to the judgment of this world and its standards. We are not to put
our hope in the world and its riches; we are to hope in Christ's
work on our behalf.

What is your own local community like? Is it a secure shelter
for those who have been ravaged by the enemy? Is it a home to
which people can retreat and let down their barriers? Is it a

harmonious place of sound teaching and godly living? These signs of loving each other will make a difference.

On the systemic or cultural front, the working out of what it means to love each other can have dramatic impact in a culture. An amazing example of this is seen in the city of La Resistencia, Argentina.[5] In the early 1980s, the evangelical church was tiny and fragmented. Of the seventy churches, all but two were the result of splits or divisions. The disunity was palpable.

As a result of approaching the evangelization of the city from a spiritual warfare perspective, however, local pastors decided that they needed to restore unity. The Spirit led some to repent of their sin in fostering disunity. This resulted in a foot-washing ceremony in which they pledged their service to one another, and in an interdenominational communion service—a statement to Satan that they meant business!

Now united, the pastors were able to pray and work *together* to reach their city. They established over six hundred interdenominational prayer centers in neighborhoods throughout the city. They conducted city-wide evangelism campaigns, and Pentecostals baptized people who would go to Baptist churches, and Baptists baptized people who would attend charismatic congregations. The unity displayed broke the back of resistance in the community, and in two years the churches quadrupled in size. Surely this is one of God's intentions for successfully waging spiritual warfare on the systemic front.

God has supplied us with a wealth of resources to build the collection of people we call our local church into a true community. We have the Holy Spirit, who empowers and enables us to live so as to please God. We have doctrinal standards based on God's Word to evaluate spiritual events and an environment in which that evaluation can take place. We have important instructions concerning Satan's schemes that enable us to know his tactics and discern his agents. And as a community, we enjoy freedom from fear of death to come against Satan in Jesus' name.

11

Putting on God's Armor

My friend Jim had a hard life. As a young boy, he found his mother after she shot herself in a suicide attempt. In his early teen years, he began a battle with alcohol. Initially giving him an escape, it became his captor. He attended a Christian college, where he had to keep his alcoholic binges hidden from even his roommate. After college, he was diagnosed as manic-depressive, and his health forced him to return to the home of his parents, who divorced two years later. But neither parent could afford to move out, so they continued to live and battle in the same house. Jim remained trapped in the middle.

The last time I saw Jim, things had begun to look brighter. He had steady employment and had been sober for six months. He was also in love with a girl he had been dating. But just three months later I received an agonizing letter from Jim. His girlfriend had broken up with him because she couldn't handle Jim's past. He felt abandoned and lost hope. Shortly after, he took his own life.

The casualties of spiritual warfare are all around us. There are situations over which people have no control, like Jim's family environment. Many, like Jim, have their lives shredded by the enemy until they lose all hope. I believe it could have made a real difference for Jim to be assured of the reality of God's love and protection in order to fight against the despair Satan threw at him. Often we do not know what spiritual armor God has provided, or we just do not know how to effectively put it on.

The Armor

To cap off our discussion of the "putting on" disciplines of spiritual warfare, we will turn to Paul's familiar passage on spiritual armor found in Ephesians 6:10-18:

Finally, be strong in the Lord and in his mighty power. Put on the full armor of God so that you can take your stand against the devil's schemes. For our struggle is not against flesh and blood, but against the rulers, against the authorities, against the powers of this dark world and against the spiritual forces of evil in the heavenly realms. Therefore put on the full armor of God, so that when the day of evil comes, you may be able to stand your ground, and after you have done everything, to stand. Stand firm then, with the belt of truth buckled round your waist, with the breastplate of righteousness in place, and with your feet fitted with the readiness that comes from the gospel of peace. In addition to all this, take up the shield of faith, with which you can extinguish all the flaming arrows of the evil one. Take the helmet of salvation and the sword of the Spirit, which is the word of God. And pray in the Spirit on all occasions with all kinds of prayers and requests. With this in mind, be alert and always keep on praying for all the saints.

Paul tells us to be strong *in the Lord,* not in our own power. The reasons are obvious. When we are strong in our own power, we are telling God we do not need him. He will quickly remind us that we really do! Paul also says that we have a role to play in this battle. It is up to us to put on the armor of God.

Thus, while we rely on God, we also are engaged in the battle. The terms Paul uses show it is a no-holds-barred wrestling match. Spiritual warfare in this sense is not a relaxed community flicking a bothersome mosquito off its arm; it is grimy, sweaty, hand-to-hand combat in which no quarter is given or taken without a struggle. In this struggle, our community of faith is to hold its position despite the temptation to change, retreat, or backtrack in light of the onslaught. Victory is assured as long as we depend on God's power rather than our own and as long as we keep God's perspective. God says our struggle is not against people but against the spirits that drive things behind the scenes.

Many people have written on the six pieces of armor that Paul details. He was in jail as he wrote this letter, and he may have even been sitting between two soldiers and used their uniforms as inspiration for his message. Paul was able to take his bad circumstances and use them to teach us about godly living; *that* is spiritual warfare at its best!

This list of armor is illustrative rather than exhaustive. Paul is not trying to say everything he can about spiritual armor. Instead he is reminding his friends at Ephesus about the things he taught them while he lived and worked among them. For example, Paul does not mention loving God as a part of the armor, but its importance for spiritual warfare cannot be denied. Many commentaries focus on the physical details of the Roman armor at that time. But rather than discussing the length of the swords or the type of shield or how shoes were made, we will zero in on the importance of Paul's concerns and how to use the armor he discusses.

To help you avoid confusion over the physical imagery, think of the armor as a single ring of interlocking puzzle pieces. If any one piece is missing, there is a gaping hole in the ring. No single piece is more valuable than any other; *each one* is necessary to maintain the integrity of the ring. It is through these holes that the "flaming arrows" of Satan enter and find their mark. Each time they land, they produce a handle for him to hold and slow down our growth or discourage us. Jesus once said that Satan had no hold on him (John 14:30); our goal in putting on the armor is to be as slippery to Satan as Jesus was!

Putting on the armor of God applies at each front of spiritual warfare. Just as soldiers need to check their armor every time they go into battle, so we must regularly assess our own need of spiritual armor. Putting on the armor as individuals, we are able to help each other. Protected by each other, our church can be strengthened and can grow in grace to stand. Just as the leaders in an army must ensure that all units are equipped and trained in using their equipment, so must the church community oversee the needs of each member. If enough churches are wearing their armor, the culture that surrounds them will not be able to swallow them up so easily. Instead, they will act as yeast in bread, spreading godly influence throughout the system and helping the system itself be molded more in the direction of God's truth.

As you read about each piece of armor, spend time in prayer. Ask God to show you ways your armor has slipped and how it can be put back on again. Let him speak to you about wearing the armor in every area of spiritual warfare.

Armed with Truth

Because Satan's very nature is to lie, truth is our first line of defense and offense. This includes doctrinal truth but is not limited to it. We are to *know* the truths of the Scripture, but we are also to *live* out truthful lives. Lying, unfaithfulness, dishonesty, rumors, and gossip undermine our claim to be people of the truth and expose us to Satan's schemes.

One of the areas of struggle for me is that I focus so much on myself, and then I lie to myself about what I am doing. I either deny it ("I am not self-absorbed; I just don't know who else to talk about!") or justify it ("If I don't look out for me, who will?"). To put on truth, I must ask God to reveal to me where I have lived a lie. I must be willing to be exposed and allow that searing exposure to burn out the ways I lie and cheat not only myself but others as well. I must learn how to see myself, not from my perspective or from the perspectives of others, but from the perspective of God. This must be done through the lens of his merciful acceptance of me, warts and all.

In addition to being truthful with myself, I must be a person of truth on the interpersonal front. Relating to each other the wonderful truths of the Word of God is half of the story. The remaining half is in encouraging, and if necessary rebuking, others to become people of integrity as well. To do this, however, I must be open to their encouragement and rebuke in my life.

Do you have a friend with whom you can engage in this type of relationship? I am blessed to have a friend with whom I can be completely myself and open to encouragement, correction, and rebuke. He challenges me as he encourages me, and together we are learning how to be truthful with God, with ourselves, and with each other.

We are to be a truthful community that demonstrates integrity and faithfulness, and we are to speak out even in a culture that denies that truth exists. That is particularly hard for Christians in the United States. A 1991 *Newsweek* survey indicated that 91 percent of those surveyed admitted lying at times. (And I'd be very surprised if the remaining 9 percent told the truth in the survey!) Another survey in the same year conducted on behalf of the Girl Scouts of America indicated that 65 percent of the fourth- to twelfth-graders surveyed said they would cheat on a major exam. A 1993 *Boston Globe* survey of college-age students found that 75 percent admitted to having cheated while in high school. As far as the churches go, George Barna's 1991 research indicated that fewer than half of our evangelical church members agree that there is an absolute truth.

A church that does not believe in truth will be hard-pressed to proclaim it with much conviction to a culture that is given over to relativism and is skeptical of any claims of absolute truth. The culture is blind to the fact that a denial of absolute truth is a claim of the very thing it denies. Our challenge until Christ returns will be to find creative ways to bring truth into the view of our culture. This can be done only if we are people of integrity and if our churches are communities of integrity.

Armed with Righteousness

As Christians we have been given Christ's righteousness; therefore, we are to live as a righteous community, showing that we are children of God and not children of rebellion. That means we honor God as Creator, live by God's standards, and refuse to yield to temptation. Our righteousness is to permeate our personal lifestyle so that we are not given to sensuality (whether lust, gluttony, or materialism). We do not live looking forward to winning the lottery but looking forward to eternity with Christ.

On the personal front, we are to know that we have been given Christ's righteousness *and* to live out what that means day by day. This does not include religious haughtiness. It does include a humble lifestyle that others see as in tune with God's way of living. It's been said that "the only Jesus many people see is the Jesus lived out in me." So we must ask ourselves: *If I claim to follow Christ, what Jesus does my life display to those who know me, who talk with me, who deal with me on a regular basis?* This right living comes not out of legalistic self-discipline but out of the overflow of a relationship with a living and loving God. It does not focus on the "do nots" of life but on the positive attitudes and actions that are to characterize the follower of Jesus.

We are also to don the armor of righteousness on the interpersonal front. This means "wearing" the qualities of Christ in our relationships with each other, which evidence his ways of relating to people. On the local church front as a community of believers, we must live lives that reflect our status as a righteous people. Anthropologists tell us that morality has no meaning outside the culture that defines it. Biologists tell us that morals are an extension of our animal instincts. Sociologists tell us there are no norms for good conduct, only descriptions of how a given people act. Philosophers argue that morality depends on a person's motives or the results achieved. Psychologists tell us that morality is whatever builds your self-esteem and empowers you as a person—or, alternately, that moral systems are little more than the source of guilt complexes and neuroses.

A Christian approach to living out righteousness should include the whole range of ethical issues from ministering to the destitute to speaking out against social injustice. With love and boldness, we need to act against structures in our society that perpetuate injustice and enslave people. Each action in these areas works against Satan's desire to dominate and destroy people through the systems he controls. Each is a reminder of the church's defiance against his lordship on earth. Each raises a banner that proclaims delight in God's ways.

Armed with Peace

Many of us have a hard time experiencing peace. The hectic pace of life gets in the way. Or maybe we're restless inside because we don't feel reconciled within ourselves. Truth and peace work together. Knowing the truth of who we are, we can begin to connect with the God who made us and experience the peace that comes from being beloved members of God's eternal family.

On the larger world front we see anything but peace around us. From Bosnia to Indonesia to Rwanda, nation after nation suffers with war, ethnic cleansings, genocide, and massive corruption—Satan's tools. Here the church can work behind the scenes for reconciliation. We can publicly sponsor invitations for fighting factions to come together and talk. But godly peace goes beyond conciliation. We are to take the offensive in sharing the gospel of Christ, because reconciling people to God is the first step in reconciling them to each other. We are to be a peaceful people who communicate the Good News to others: they can have peace with God and with others!

Armed with Faith

David Lloyd-Jones defines *faith* as "the ability to apply quickly what we believe so as to repel everything the devil does or attempts to do to us."[1] As we exercise our trust in God's power, God enables us to extinguish the evil one's flaming darts. The faith we have, of course, stems from the work of the Spirit in us individually and as a community.

For fourteen years, as a staff member of a faith-supported organization, I saw God supply my every need. During that span, I married, and we had three children. God always provided. His faithfulness has continued since we returned home and have added a fourth child. In spite of a track record in my own life that stretches back over the past twenty years, I still struggle with believing he will meet our needs on a day-to-day basis. When we found termites in our house last summer, I worried. When our hot-water heater started leaking, I worried. When the children need clothes, I worry. If I am to put on the shield of faith, I must commit myself to trust God, not in a general sense, but in the specifics of daily life.

Interpersonally, we can help one another trust in God's ongoing work in our lives. My wife has been an encouragement to me, helping me see that what I want to label as "responsibility" is all too often simply unnecessary and even sinful worrying. She has a far more intact faith in God's provisions than I do. At times I get angry about it, wishing she would worry more! Then I realize that I am wishing to pull her down to my level of faith rather than letting God use her to pull me up to her ability to relax in God's faithfulness.

On the local church front, our faith communities are to trust

God to meet our needs, whether that pertains to budgets, leadership needs, physical facilities, or spiritual growth. A huge temptation in many Western cultures is to trust our planning techniques, our conflict-resolution skills, our budgeting expertise. None of these are evil, but all can be used as a replacement for faith that God has all plans in his capable hands, that he is the ultimate resolver of conflict, and that he owns the earth and all in it. Exercising that faith keeps Satan's attacks from having the devastating impact he wants to have.

On the systemic front, faith is directed in God's sovereign control in spite of the way things may look on the surface. We live in a century that has produced more martyrs for the Christian faith than all prior centuries. It is estimated that at least 150,000 people lose their lives because of their faith every year. Even in the face of that staggering statistic, and often in countries where the death rate is the highest, the church is growing. The faithful peace of those martyred often stands as a testimony to unbelievers that there is something substantive to the Christian life that they do not have. It is the type of faith that the very gates of hell shall never prevail against.

Armed with the Hope of Salvation

The fifth weapon we have is hope in our salvation. We can rest in the fact that our names are written in the Book of Life and that Satan can do nothing about it. We also can rest in the fact that the future is sealed, and victory belongs to Christ. Our assurance of salvation enables us to see earthly circumstances in proper perspective. With this hope engaged, we may still fear the fact of experiencing death, but the consequences of death need no longer drive our actions. And people free of the fear of death are empowered to do whatever God calls them to do.

I see this area attacked in people's lives on a regular basis.

Whenever Satan can cause us to lose our hope, he has significant ground in our lives to work. Proverbs states, "Hope deferred makes the heart sick" (13:12). Jim, mentioned at the beginning of this chapter, was a spiritual warfare casualty. A chief means of attack on him was hopeless despair. We are to rest in the hope we have in Christ not only for salvation but also in his promise to eventually right the wrongs that have been committed against us.

When my hope flags, it is the hope of brothers and sisters in Christ from which I draw strength. When their hope flags, they can draw on mine. Attacks on our hope should not be seen as limited to flesh and blood. They are demonically inspired, and recognizing the source will help us face the real enemy. I'm afraid I didn't recognize what Jim was facing as spiritual warfare, and the platitudes I offered did not help him reframe what was happening to him.

On the local church front, we are to train people to rest in God's secure hope. We preach hope to ourselves, reminding each other where our hope comes from and on whom it depends. We serve as outposts of hope to a world that is either becoming increasingly hopeless or is building hope on false foundations.

It is our hope of God's eventual victory that gives us the strength to fight the battles against injustice and the evil structures in our societies that dehumanize people. While we may despair of establishing truly just societies prior to the return of Christ, we may still erect pockets of justice within those societies that will serve before the world as pointers to God's priorities in life. May our churches wear the hope of Christ as vibrantly as Paul did: "We are hard pressed on every side, but not crushed; perplexed, but not in despair; persecuted, but not abandoned; struck down, but not destroyed. We always carry around in our body the death of Jesus, so that the life of Jesus may also be revealed in our body" (2 Cor. 4:8-10).

Armed with Spirit-Led Words

The last weapon Paul mentions is our sword, which *The New English Bible* translates as "the words that come from God." When we find ourselves in a spiritual struggle, the Spirit gives us the words to battle with, but *we* must say them. Remember Jesus' temptation? He responded to Satan's proposals by quoting Scripture, the words of God. His verbal proclamation of the truth of Scripture enabled him to resist the enemy's challenges. The same is true for us.

A woman was having problems with her child, whose behavior was wild and uncontrollable. Once, when the child was crying inconsolably, she prayed out loud, "The weapons we fight with are not the weapons of this world. On the contrary, they have divine power to demolish strongholds" (2 Cor. 10:4). Then she commanded Satan to leave her child alone. The child immediately quieted down. In a practical way, this is taking up the sword of the Spirit.

Our fear, of course, is that either we will be seen as crazy or we will be addressing spooks who aren't really there. Satan loves to play on these fears. He pushes us to the extremes of seeing every problem as a demon or of ignoring the demonic altogether. Demons are *not* the cause of every problem. Neither are they dormant, inactive, or nonexistent. The key is to live to please God, then speak as he leads.

On the personal level, using the sword of God's Word requires that we use what we have memorized in the circumstances of life. These can be used as prayers to God, reminders to ourselves, or pronouncements to the enemy of our intention to walk as godly people. On the interpersonal front, we may use Scripture defensively to fight off Satan's attacks with truth. Offensively, we are to comfort or confront people with words of truth. At the local church level, Scripture forms the foundation for sermons, public prayer, and the exercise of the verbal gifts. On the systemic front, the sword of God's Word is wielded in the many ways we may bring God's truth into the public arena, whether through politics, media, books, music, or art.

Energized through Prayer

All of our battle gear is to be put on in a spiritual atmosphere of prayer. Prayer is certainly the power source behind all of the weapons we have been given. In an attitude of humility and obedience, we come to God in prayer, asking for insight into chinks in our armor, confessing sin. Prayerfully, we take up each piece. The following questions may serve as guidelines for you in this sort of prayer.

Truth: How have I been untruthful? In what circumstances today might my integrity be tested? What are creative ways I can display the truth of God as a living force in my life?

Righteousness: Where have I fallen short of God's way of living? What can I do to be ready for temptations in this area? What are loving ways I can show the righteousness of God?

Peace: Is there anyone with whom I am not at peace? How can I share God's peace in some constructive way with him or her today?

Faith: Where have I been unfaithful or lost my own faith? How might I be tempted to not trust God today? What truth do I need to face the tests?

Hope of Salvation: In what areas have I lost sight of the hope God has planted in my heart? In what ways am I trying to earn my salvation, which has been given as a gift? How can I bring hope to others?

Spirit-Led Words: What parts of God's Word have I hidden in my heart? What situations will I face today in which God's Word will help me stand against the evil one? What keeps me from using the "sword of the Spirit" in my life?

While many of us understand the need for prayer on the

personal level, it has only been in the past two decades that the worldwide church has begun to awaken to the need for and power in public prayer. Korea is leading the way. Many Korean churches have bought small mountains and turned them into prayer retreats. They schedule several early-morning prayer services to accommodate all who want to attend. There is little doubt that the explosive growth in Korean churches and missionary work is due to their work in corporate prayer.

In this section we have selectively discussed the relationship of spiritual disciplines to spiritual warfare. We saw that it is essential to identify sin and deal with it. On the positive side, we are to cultivate a love relationship with God and with each other. We are also to prayerfully put on spiritual armor. Some say that these things are all we need to do. However, the biblical perspective is clear that knowing truth and applying spiritual disciplines are not the whole picture. Another essential part of being fully equipped for warfare is understanding and exercising our authority in Christ, the focus of the next section.

III.
Standing Firm

12

The Christian's Authority

Shirley was struggling when she came to see me. She was afraid to seek help because she truly thought that demons would take over the process. Her fear was built on the underlying assumption that demons were really in control. As we talked through some things, she found that she *could* rest in the fact that she belonged to God. Nothing strange happened, and the process was not "taken over" by demons. Instead, Shirley confessed that she had let fear dominate her, examined how fear had infiltrated her life, and announced her resolve to trust and fear God rather than the enemy. Now she finds that God is replacing her fear with peace.

We have come to the most controversial area of spiritual warfare: the Christian's authority over Satan. I have purposely chosen to discuss this area last because it must be framed in context. In exploring the issue of spiritual warfare, it is all too easy to focus on the sensational and ignore the need for a basis of understanding and applying truth, stripping off sin, and putting on godliness. Without those foundations, however, exercising Christian authority over the enemy can become an exercise in frustration, delusion, or even paranoia.

At the same time, there will be moments in our lives when we must apply God's truth by exercising the authority he has given us to confront the enemy's challenge. And it is not just a matter of believing the right things. As James noted, even the demons believe in God and his power, and they shudder in fear about it (James 2:19). Standing firm involves *acting* on our faith to come against the attacks of Satan.

Satan's Limits

Before we discuss issues of the Christian's authority, however, a word of caution is in order. As we discovered in chapter 5, Satan is a limited creature. If he were personally responsible for all that is attributed to him by Christians today, he would have to be everywhere and know everything. That is simply not the case. Being limited, he is forced to let demons do the vast bulk of his work. It is they who harass, tempt, hinder, thwart, and influence people.

Can Satan read our minds, or is that limited, too? Scripture presents no clear statements on the issue. Some feel that he cannot read our minds because he is not omniscient. While it is true that God alone knows everything, this does not mean that Satan cannot read our thoughts. It only means that his knowledge is limited, while God's is unlimited. As far as I can see, the possibility that he can read our thoughts cannot be proven or denied on a scriptural basis. But even if he cannot read our minds, he and his demons have had uncounted millennia studying humanity. Thus, even if direct mind reading is not possible, demonic ability to "read us like a book" cannot be discounted.

Some feel uncomfortable with the idea that Satan can read our thoughts. However, if God thought this was an important issue for us to know, he would have put a definite statement about it somewhere in his Word. Our focus should not be on keeping secrets from Satan but in walking in the light with God and fellow believers. We should not be overly concerned with our ability to outthink or outstrategize him, or worry too much that if he knows something about us he will have new power over us. Recognize that your fears, secret vices, and nightmares are known to demons simply because they closely watch all people in order to tempt, blind, intimidate, and destroy them. The issue is not whether they know your secrets but whether you are allowing their knowledge to intimidate you. Do not be frightened by the idea that demons might know your thoughts. Instead, fill your mind with godly thoughts so completely that they will not *want* to know what you're thinking!

The Foundation for Resisting Satan

Victory in spiritual warfare does not come to the proud and self-sufficient. Two Bible passages directly command us to resist Satan by going on the offensive: humbling ourselves toward God and standing firm in the faith (1 Pet. 5:5-10; James 4:6-7). Jesus warned that we would have to take up our cross, deny ourselves, and follow him (Matt. 16:24-26). Theologian Walter Wink captures the essential attitude: "Jesus does not ask for more self-denial. . . . It is not a question of denying certain things to oneself, like ice cream during Lent, but of *disowning* the ego's claim to possess this life. The task is not ego-conquest . . . but ego-surrender to the redemptive initiatives of God."[1] Without a foundation of humility and submission to God, people can too easily think of themselves as "Christian Green Berets," relying on tactics that are little different from the enemy's. There is no need to seek out attacks; plenty will come our way if we are living as God wants us to live. This is why some Christians have trouble with the very term *spiritual warfare*. While they acknowledge the battle, they rightfully point out (as we discussed in chapter 6) that the experience of peace with God and others is our ultimate goal, rather than the battle itself.

No Exemptions

Many Christians hope to find ways to avoid Satan's attacks. If anyone had a right to expect that he had full protection against the enemy, it was Job. He was a righteous man, we are told, and he carefully dealt with his own sins and the sins of his family (Job 1:5). When Satan wanted to attack him, he felt there was a hedge around Job that kept him spiritually "safe"—a hedge of wealth. When the wealth was removed, Satan proposed that Job would immediately give up his faith (1:11).

Paul, too, might have expected to avoid Satan's attacks. As his second letter to the Corinthians makes clear, however, one of the worst attacks was allowed by God as a kind of preventive medicine for pride:

> To keep me from becoming conceited because of these sur-passingly great revelations, there was given me a thorn in my flesh, *a messenger of Satan,* to torment me. Three times I pleaded with the Lord to take it away from me. But he said to me, 'My grace is sufficient for you, for my power is made perfect in weakness.' Therefore I will boast all the more gladly about my weaknesses, so that Christ's power may rest on me." (2 Cor. 12:7-9, emphasis mine)

Righteous living does not exempt us from further sufferings. We will stumble and we will face trials. There is no sure-fire preven-tion or prescription to stop demonic bombardment. But though we cannot prevent the attacks, we can resist them by keeping our focus on God and our identity in Christ. We can also rest in the assurance that if (or when) we fail, God will still be able to restore us.

Authority for the Battle

What is the extent of the Christian's authority over demons? The authority Jesus exercised was delegated to his twelve disciples (Matt. 10:1, 8) and others, who were successful in setting people free in Jesus' name (Mark 9:38-41). Today, some argue that this authority was limited to the apostles and is no longer available for Christians. This idea, however, goes against the grain of Paul's teaching.

Paul builds the foundation of spiritual warfare on the basis of our identity in Christ, a theme interwoven throughout Ephesians. In chapter 1, Paul prays that his readers would understand God's power that is working on their behalf. This power raised Christ from the dead and put all things under Christ's dominion. Having expressed this prayer, Paul reminds the Ephesian Christians that they once had been dead in their sins but have now been made alive in Christ. He then states: "But because of his great love for us, God, who is rich in mercy, made us alive with Christ even when we were dead in transgressions—it is by grace you have been saved. And God raised us up with Christ and *seated us with him in the heavenly realms* in Christ Jesus" (Eph. 2:4-6, emphasis mine).

Christ is above all authorities, and we sit with him in the position of honor and authority at God's right hand. Clearly, Christians participate in the authority of Christ. An example of this is seen in Acts 16:18, when Paul commands a demon to leave a slave girl whom it had enabled to prophesy. The context shows that she had been following them for several days, obnoxiously announcing that Paul and his companions were "God's messengers." Paul finally got annoyed at this and commanded the demon to leave. There was no battle, only the single command with instant obedience.

Why Paul waited for several days before acting we do not really know. Perhaps he did not initially know it was a demonic announcement. After all, she certainly drew attention to Paul and to the gospel, which he probably welcomed. In any event, when he tired of her constant shouting, he simply stated, "In the name of Jesus Christ, I command you to come out of her." He addressed the demon directly. His use of "in the name of Jesus Christ" is not a ritual formula but a way of life for one fully

submitted to Christ's lordship. By this Paul shows his awareness
that he was simply accessing the power and authority of Christ.

At the same time, it should be noted that our ability to exercise
our authority is not completely without constraints. As we noted,
Paul was unsuccessful in having his "thorn in the flesh" removed
because God had better plans than healing. Our exercise of
Christ's authority remains under God's sovereign hand.

Can We Bind Satan?

There is a lively debate about the Christian's ability to "bind
Satan." Some say we have no right to use this type of language.
Others seem ready to bind Satan at the drop of a hat. Many of us
have heard prayers that seek to bind Satan's influence over
people, meetings, Bible studies, crusades, television broadcasts,
electronic equipment, and so on. Because the debate is so heated,
it is worth a deeper look at what the Bible teaches about
binding evil.[2]

In the Bible's original language, the word *deo* (*to bind*) means
"to constrain in some way." This might be done physically or
nonphysically. Physically, it could refer to tying up wheat at
harvesttime (Matt. 13:30), tethering a donkey (Matt. 21:2),
subduing someone with ropes or chains (Matt. 14:3; Acts 12:6),
or wrapping a body for burial (John 11:44; 19:40).

Nonphysical binding might be accomplished legally, emotionally, psychologically, socially, culturally, or spiritually.
Again, the central idea is a constraint that limits a person.
Husband and wife, for example, are "bound" to each other (Rom.
7:2; 1 Cor. 7:27). This binding is legal in the mutual legal rights
and obligations, emotional in the love relationship, psychological in the common pursuit of a successful marriage, social in the
sense that there are limitations on their sexual relationships with
others (e.g., sexual fidelity), and spiritual in the sense of the two
being one in God's sight.

It is the *spiritual sense of binding* that is important in spiritual warfare. This binding ranges from restraint in a limited situation to total control. There are six examples of this use of the word *bind* in the Bible.

1) After freeing a man from the power of demons and being accused of doing it through Satan's power, Jesus tells a parable of binding the strong man and plundering his house (Matt. 12:22-29). This binding enables the house to be plundered, but only those who accept the freedom Jesus offers experience the liberation that the binding allows. Those who reject it remain Satan's captives.

2) Jesus freed a woman who had been bound with a physical illness by Satan for eighteen years (Luke 13:16). She stands as an example of one taken from Satan's house. Satan bound her physically and emotionally. When she placed her faith in Jesus for release, Satan himself was restrained from continuing to work in her life, and her deepest desire was granted.

3) Jesus told Peter and the disciples that whatever they bound or loosed on earth has been bound or loosed in heaven (Matt. 16:18-19 and 18:18-20). Both passages have been the subject of extensive scholarly debate. I understand these verses to express our task as Christians to proclaim Christ and open the kingdom of God to those who will receive it, as well as to close it from those who reject it. As an extension of Jesus' strong-man metaphor, we plunder Satan's "house" through evangelism and releasing people from demonization, though the people themselves must choose to accept release.

4) Paul was bound in the Spirit, or constrained by God's direction, to go to Jerusalem (Acts 20:22). Though constrained, Paul still had to choose to obey the constraint. In this instance, the church was telling him that he should not go because of what waited for him there. He, however, knew that God wanted him to go, so he could not obey the urging of the church.

5) In the end times, four angels who are bound will be released

to kill one-third of the earth's population (Rev. 9:14). The constraining force here is obviously God. It is limited only in the sense that in God's timing it will be withdrawn and the angels' destructive forces will be experienced.

6) Satan will be bound with a chain and confined to a locked pit for one thousand years (Rev. 20:1-3). This binding of Satan, though complete in the amount of restraint, is also limited in time. His final binding, though the word is not used, comes when he meets his eternal judgment in the lake of fire (Rev. 20:10).

These instances of spiritual restraint show the types of spiritual binding that the term can be used to describe. In answering the question "Can Christians bind Satan?" then, it is important to know what people mean by the term. It obviously cannot mean that we can constrain him from all activities, or else Peter's command to be alert to his attacks would not make sense. On the other hand, if by binding Satan we mean limiting, hindering, constraining, and even stopping his work in the lives of others, then Christians certainly *can* bind him.

Such binding is accomplished through the exercise of authority. However, the binding will only be as effective as the authority of the one who binds. This helps us understand what it means for Christians to bind Satan. We exercise *Christ's authority,* which has been granted to us to hinder and restrain Satan's work in our lives and the lives of others, an authority grounded in Jesus' incarnation, life, death, and resurrection.

There are some restrictions in our binding Satan that naturally arise out of the character of God and the nature of our relationship with God through Christ. First, it is God's authority we exercise, and he will permit only that which is consistent with his will. Paul did pray for the thorn in the flesh to be removed, but God clearly said no, because he had a greater purpose in mind.

The second restriction in binding Satan is the state of our relationship with God. Only his children can access his authority.

This is clearly seen in the unsuccessful attempt to expel demons by the Jewish exorcists in Acts 19. They failed because, in spite of using Christ's name, they did not have a relationship with him. In addition, sin and self-reliance hinder our ability to access God's authority (Mark 9:14-29).

In conclusion, binding Satan is an application of exercising the authority we have in Christ, and the same constraints that apply to our exercise of authority also apply to binding. These constraints are not designed to set us up for failure. Instead, they force us to focus on our relationship with Christ rather than on a simple "name it and claim it" philosophy that places God in the position of simply servicing our commands. We are privileged to bind Satan, but this is not a cavalier privilege to be used on a whim. When we bind Satan, we are to be reminded of Christ's awesome work on the cross and that our access to the victory he won is only by God's continuing grace at work in our lives.

We Are Privileged!

As followers of Jesus we are in a privileged position. We sit with Christ at the right hand of God in the heavenly realms. We are allowed to exercise his authority, but we are not to do so lightly. We also participate in his work of binding the enemy by sharing the Good News and setting people free from demonic control. The practical work of exercising our authority in Christ on every front of spiritual warfare is the subject we now turn to. Before you read on, however, take some time to prayerfully reflect on the privilege it is to be a child of God. Commit yourself to be faithful in battle, and find creative ways to hinder Satan's work to deceive, dominate, and destroy you and others.

13

Fighting the Good Fight

When our daughter Lauren was about one year old, she started waking up at night screaming. Being our first child, we were not sure what to make of it. She had always been a peaceful sleeper, a fact for which we had been deeply grateful! The problem was that these were not cries of hunger. They were screams, and we had no idea what caused them.

After a week, my wife, Emily, told me that she had read somewhere that children might start to experience bad dreams at Lauren's age. Realizing that one possible source of bad dreams is the intimidating work of Satan, we decided to take our stance. That night, as we put Lauren to bed, we prayed over her. We thanked God for her and for our relationship with him. We announced to the enemy that he had no ground to stand on and that we were claiming our authority in Christ over our daughter. We declared that if the dreams were from Satan, they had to stop. They did! From that night on, Lauren slept peacefully.

What happened so impressed us that we began to pray over our own dreams as well. We simply ask God to be glorified in our dreams and come against any attempts to use them to intimidate us. I have seen a dramatic change in my dreams. Now, I almost never have nightmares. Our children rarely have them either. I'm sure that part of that is due to the fact that we limit their television viewing and don't let them watch horror movies. But I am also convinced that the ability to claim God's authority over our dreams is a protection that is available to us as Christians, though many in the West discount this as an option. Until we saw what happened with Lauren, we discounted it as well!

Overpowering Evil with Good

How can we fight the good fight? We must start with the right attitude. There is a story that one day Satan visited Martin Luther with a long scroll in his hand. He said to Luther, "Here I have a list of the sins you have committed. I want to show it to you." On seeing the list, Luther asked if that was all. Satan produced a second scroll. Again Luther asked if that was all, and again Satan produced another scroll. After repeating this several times, Satan finally admitted that there were no more scrolls. Luther said to him, "Look at all the things that Christ died for just for me! How great are his grace and mercy on my behalf. As for you, Satan—get out of here!" The enemy fled, and Luther went on his way rejoicing.

Luther took Satan's best shot and turned it to God's advantage. This is what Paul commands: overpower evil with good (Rom. 12:21). We are called to put as much energy as we can into thinking up ways to use good to "surprise" and overcome evil. Let's get practical. When someone speaks ill of you, discipline yourself to count it as a blessing instead. When someone wrongs you, learn how to forgive and not seek revenge. When you face the reality of your own sin, turn it to confession, repentance, and praise to God for his promised forgiveness. When you are attacked for sins committed in the past and weighed down with old guilt, begin to see those sins in the perspective of the largess of the Cross and God's forgiveness. These are the types of responses Jesus preached about in the Sermon on the Mount. To wage spiritual warfare successfully we need to discover ways to take the offensive and overpower evil with good.

Capturing Your Thoughts

In what is a combination of discipline and authority, Paul instructs us that our thought life is important:

> For though we live in the world, we do not wage war as the world does. The weapons we fight with are not the weapons of the world. On the contrary, they have divine power to demolish strongholds. We demolish arguments and every pretension that sets itself up against the knowledge of God, and we take captive every thought to make it obedient to Christ. (2 Cor. 10:3-5)

Think of the strongholds Paul mentions as thought patterns burned into our minds through habit or traumatic experience. In effect, they are the mental programs by which we operate, and they reveal themselves in un-Christlike temperaments and behavior. By making our thoughts obedient to Christ, such patterns can be destroyed and replaced with behaviors that glorify God.

Paul doesn't mean that we have to monitor and control every stray thought that comes into our heads. But when evil thoughts do come, we can simply choose to ignore them and move on. When we find ourselves dwelling on these thoughts, we should "take them captive" to the throne of Christ. Here is how I personally do this: I close my eyes, cup my hands, and imagine placing the thought in my hands. I lift my hands up to God, asking if the thoughts are pleasing in his sight. I then announce my rejection of those thoughts that are not pleasing to God. As with confession of sins, this discipline takes time to cultivate. You may want to develop your own way to shape the habit of watching over your thoughts.

Moving to the community and systemic fronts of our warfare, Satan's strongholds are those cultural patterns and assumptions that dominate our culture—including the church. For example,

Christians know that materialism is wrong, but we can find hundreds of ways to justify our culture's relentless pursuit of material goods as a means of finding satisfaction in life. All too often, this is because we ourselves have been caught up in it. In our own lives and in the church, our task is to identify ungodly strongholds so that we can act as a leavening influence in the larger culture.

Overcoming with Authority

We saw in chapter 11 that believers have authority over Satan through the power of the Cross and God's Word. But how much verbal authority we have is debated. In Revelation 12:11, we discover that Satan is overcome in part by the "testimony of believers." The word *testimony* here means more than just our own story of coming to faith. It is the verbal proclamation of the truth of God as revealed by Jesus and as it works in our lives. Such testimony is obviously verbal. Our words aren't magical, but they are important in renouncing the works of Satan.

So where is the controversy? Jude 9 states, "But even the archangel Michael, when he was disputing with the devil about the body of Moses, did not dare to bring a slanderous accusation against him, but said, 'The Lord rebuke you!'" Some people feel this passage teaches that we must treat Satan with respect, as Michael the archangel did. While I agree that we must treat Satan within the framework of kingdom ethics, the point here is that Michael could not reject the devil's accusation against Moses (which was only slander) on his own authority. He could only ask God to condemn Satan for slander. Michael acted out of submission to God, not respect for Satan. We, too, act out of submission to God when we speak against Satan's attacks.

The saints also overcome Satan by "the blood of the Lamb" (Rev. 12:11). These words have been turned into a ritual phrase by many, who invoke "the blood of the Lamb" as if it were a talisman to ward off evil powers. Oswald Sanders remarks in his book *Satan Is No Myth:*

> "The blood of the Lamb" is not a kind of magic charm, a ritual that we import into sermon or prayer to attest to our orthodoxy or to secure supernatural results. It is not a formula to be credulously mumbled, nor is it a parroting of mystical words. It is the expression of an intelligent, active, vital faith in Christ, the Lamb of God, who by the shedding of His blood, bruised Satan's head and utterly defeated him. . . . So then, when in prayer we plead the blood of the Lamb, we are really saying that our faith is resting for victory over Satan and sin upon all that Christ achieved for us by His victorious death and victorious resurrection.[1]

Just as we are to pray "in Jesus' name," so too we can claim and rest in the finished work of the Cross that is symbolized in "the blood of the Lamb." Both are shorthand statements of personal faith and belief in, trust in, and reliance on the work of Jesus on our behalf.

Empowering Others for Battle

It all started for Linda when she asked God to give her a spirit of wisdom and revelation. Shortly afterwards, she began to hear a voice. Excitement overwhelmed her as she began to converse with what she thought was the answer to her prayer. Over the next five years, the voice multiplied; now many, they began to offer advice and predict the future. When Linda and I finally sat down together to talk over the issue, she was extremely agitated.

She explained how the voices had first started speaking to her and how they began to tell her what would happen to her in the future. Now she relied on the voices for guidance in life, believing they were coming from God. As we talked, she began to consider that perhaps they were not from God after all. When I mentioned that their intention was eventually to destroy her, she explained that they had been talking to her about that on a regular basis. The voices, which had once been friendly, were now domineering.

Linda wanted to get rid of the voices. When it came time to pray, however, she balked. "But what if they can tell me something that I need to know?" she asked. We again discussed their goal in her life. But once again, she balked when it came time to pray against them. Linda was afraid to let go of the voices. Despite the fact that they freely talked about destroying her, she had developed a dependence on them. She left my office some time later, still clinging to the idea that the voices had important information for her that she was afraid to miss.

How do we help those like Linda? More generally, what is our role in helping others meet the challenge of spiritual warfare in their own lives? How can we encourage, free, and empower them to live a life pleasing to God?

In Linda's case, many advocate that I should have claimed my authority in Christ, prayed against the demons causing the voices, and cast them out of her. But I don't think the issue is as simple as that. If the voices were *not* demonic, I could cause Linda deep damage through a reckless power encounter. In any event, Linda *wanted* the voices. They gave her a sense of security and significance. Had the voices truly been demonic, and had they been cast out without Linda changing her attitude, they would simply have come back as soon as she left my office. Their hold would have been stronger, and her problems more severe. Ultimately, the decision was Linda's. I wish I could report otherwise, but she decided to keep these companions in spite of their stated intentions. I have not heard from her since.

Before we use the authority we have in Christ, we need to know that such encounters will *empower* the person facing the problems, not just free them. Freeing them is the means to the end, not the end in itself. The old adage applies: "Give a man a fish and you feed him for a day; teach a man to fish, and you feed him for life." Continuing the metaphor, sometimes we must first give a fish so that the person will gain the strength to learn how *to* fish. There are times when teaching someone how to claim their own authority in Christ is an important *first* step in helping them begin to grow in their relationship with him.

Tom was having trouble with his dream life. His dreams were not just weird. He felt a presence in the room, sometimes crushing his chest and making it impossible to breathe. A friend told him that leaving his Bible open on the bedside table would help. Tom tried it, and it did help, but only for a few days. Eventually Tom tried opening the Bible to Mark 5, the account of the demoniac released by Jesus. That helped, but again only for a few days. Finally, Tom began to place the Bible under his pillow. That, too, proved to be a temporary remedy. By the time Tom and I talked, he had experienced more than one hundred night visitations in a two-year period.

As he explained his struggle, it was obvious that he was using the Bible in a magical way, rather than resting in his authority in Christ. We decided that the best course of action was to begin a discipline of praying about his dreams when going to bed at night. That night he prayed for God's protection over his dream life. He claimed Christ's authority over his life and commanded the enemy to leave him alone. That night, and for the next two weeks, he slept peacefully. Later, when an evil dream did come back, he was not intimidated by it. He could "fish" for himself now. Over the course of the next few years, the dreams came less and less frequently. Now Tom is not bothered by them.

His exercise was not simply replacing one type of "magic" with another. Rather, it was a simple declaration of who he was in Christ, and that Satan's intimidation tactics would no longer work.

Spiritual versus Psychological

The question of whether demonic problems are physical or psychological is still unresolved. Even within Christian circles there are conflicting reports from both sides of the issue. Paul Meier, a well-known Christian psychiatrist, writes that he rarely meets a person who hears voices, who does not have the voices disappear after a few days of antipsychotic medicine. Neil Anderson reports that many who have been hearing voices have found their freedom not through medication but by walking through the "Steps to Freedom" that he has developed based on spiritual truths.

A world view that can *hold ideas in tension* will allow both explanations to be accepted and challenged within their contexts. It avoids the danger of reducing all phenomena to a single explanation. It also gives room to explore new explanations. Can people hear voices because of chemical imbalances in the brain? Apparently they can. Can people unconsciously generate voices to speak forth needs that they are consciously suppressing to meet psychological needs? Apparently they can. Can they also unconsciously generate those voices to alleviate social tensions? Apparently they can. Can demons generate voices in our head for the purpose of confusing and frightening us? Apparently they can. Because one explanation works in certain instances does not mean that other explanations are wrong. No single explanation will apply to every case in every culture of the world for all time. Both sides can learn from each other.

Enduring the attacks of Satan is common to Christians. When we undergo pressure from the enemy, we need not think that we are being singled out. We can take solace in the fact that our own suffering is something that other Christians also face. If nothing else, this should give us encouragement to share our burdens with other members of the body of Christ, knowing that they, too, face attacks. As we learn and grow together, we become stronger as a body in resisting the enemy. At the same time, we are empowered to exercise our authority and resist the enemy so that he will flee.

One weekend, while living in Kenya, Emily and I had taken some time off in a local hotel to plan, pray, and enjoy some time alone together. On Saturday night, as we were preparing to go to dinner, she came out of the bathroom hunched over. She looked up at me and said in a barely audible voice, "Pray. I can't breathe." I saw the panicked look on her face. Her lips were blue. In the past, Emily had been hospitalized several times for her allergy-related asthma. But our hotel was forty-five minutes from the nearest hospital, and Kenya has no 911 service. This was the worst attack she had ever had. She sat down on the bed, exhausted just from trying to breathe. She couldn't even breathe enough to use her inhaler.

I prayed. I renounced the attack as from the enemy, and together we resisted his attempt on her life. She vividly remembers thinking that this was her time to die. God began to release Emily from the squeeze of the asthma attack. Carefully we left the hotel, got into our car, and began the drive to the hospital. Halfway there, she turned to me and said, "I don't need to go to the hospital anymore." Her breathing was completely normal again. God had heard our cries and responded. Together we had resisted, and the enemy had fled.

Authority in the Local Church

Neil Anderson invites people to play a game to bring the reality of spiritual warfare down to earth. I have adapted it here for you or a group to work through.[2]

Imagine that you are Satan. Your goal is to blind non-Christians and to stop Christians from sharing their faith with others. Whenever possible, you want to destroy the work of God.

Unfortunately (from your perspective), you are not everywhere at once. You are, however, the leader of a host of demons who obey you and help you in your cause. In your meanderings, you notice a church that is growing. People are coming to Christ, and Christians are building a sense of community among themselves. Even the non-Christians in the city are starting to talk about what the church is doing. Given that scenario, how will you deploy your troops? What will you do to accomplish your goal?

What kind of ideas did you come up with? Would you assign some demons to work in the community, finding ways to spread rumors about the church? Did you delegate to some the responsibility of getting people in the church to start bickering, perhaps over decisions related to a new building program? Did you look for people in the community you could influence to go into the church to stir up problems? Would you try to generate pride over the growth that is taking place? What types of weaknesses would you look for?

This simple exercise can open up our thinking about Satan's strategizing. It can also open our eyes to see why the leaders of the church need to know the authority they have in Christ and how to exercise it. Church leaders are the ones to whom God gives both the responsibility and authority for acting on behalf of the church. They are not to treat that authority lightly. They are not to become dictators over the flock, lest they become satanic in their leadership. They are to ensure that the people in the church are growing in their understanding and application of truth as well as being alert to Satan's schemes within the church. On behalf of the church they are to exercise Christ's authority to repel the enemy's attacks without developing a "demon behind every problem" mentality. The church members have the responsibility to pray for their leaders, asking God to give them the wisdom and discernment needed to meet the challenges they face.

What about Territorial Spirits?

In Christian circles, the novels of Frank Peretti did not so much chart a new direction in thinking as describe the path many were already walking. His best-selling books—which vividly portray angels and demons in fierce battles over schools, towns, and whole territories—captured the imaginations of many, with *This Present Darkness* and *Piercing the Darkness* selling well in both Christian and general markets.

This reflects a cultural fascination with spirit beings, especially angels, that has grown tremendously over the past several years. Angels have been the subject of movies, television specials, and even a popular network series. Bookstore sections have been given over to books about them. On the Internet, Web sites advertise psychic angel-contacting services. Angel paraphernalia is being hawked everywhere you turn, with specialty stores focusing only on angel-related products.

Parallel to this development in our culture is the development in mission circles of a fascination with "territorial spirits." C. Peter Wagner has written in *Confronting the Powers* that by including territorial spirits as an element in ministry, we have introduced a "spiritual technology" that will bring the greatest power boost in the mission of the church since William Carey started the Protestant missions movement at the end of the eighteenth century.[3]

I hesitate to mention this issue in this chapter; it deserves far more space than we have. At the same time, the issue must be at least cursorily addressed because of its growing popularity and the potential involved.[4]

What Wagner and others call "strategic-level spiritual warfare" is praying against these territorial spirits. They seek to "map" their strategies over given locations by discerning their names and the tools they use to keep people in bondage, and then to bind them in turn so that evangelism may go unhindered. The idea of "spiritual mapping" is one in which people research an area and try to identify the spirit(s) who are in charge over it so that "smart bomb" praying may loosen the spirit's hold and enable the people there to come to Christ more freely.[5]

The idea of spirits serving over territories makes sense biblically. The only real glimpse we have of this is from Daniel 10–11, when an angel comes in answer to Daniel's prayer. That angel tells Daniel that he was delayed by the "prince of Persia," which the vast majority of commentators throughout church history has taken to be a demonic spirit working in Persia. From this and other hints (for example, the fact that the demons in Mark 5:10 did not want to leave a particular area may be significant), and the fact that Satan is limited and must distribute authority in some fashion, has come the idea of territorial spirits. Their job is to watch over selected territories (which may be geographical or ethnic) and to influence the people in that area through human instruments.

Also, one of the emphases of those engaged in this type of ministry is to discern areas in which the church needs to repent. Often this comes with a call for a public gathering to express corporate repentance. Certainly this is a positive action that unleashes the power of God to work powerfully in a location or people, and one in which we should be delighted to participate.

While we do see some room for the idea of a hierarchy of demons from Scripture, nowhere does the Bible call Christians to engage in prayer against these spirits. If this type of spiritual warfare were as significant as its advocates claim it to be, then why do we not see even a single validated example of it in Scripture? In addition to the lack of evidence from Scripture, there are no clear examples from church history.

The requirement to find the name of territorial spirits is dangerously close to Christian magic. The idea of needing the names to have power over spirits is found in magical thinking around the world. An Indian friend of mine has told me that one of the most difficult problems he now faces in witnessing to his Hindu friends is the accusation that Christians are magicians. They have observed teams of Christians coming to their region and praying against the spirits. These Hindus thus conclude that Christianity is no different from Hinduism in approaching the spirits and God. They see nothing different from what Hindu magicians practice. Though only one situation, in this case, this type of spiritual warfare has been more damaging than helpful.

Finally, the focus on prayer as a weapon against the enemy can overshadow the importance of prayer as intercession and fellowship with our Creator. Prayer was not intended to be a "smart bomb," but a means of fellowship, growth, and strength. One danger of an attitude of what has been called "spiritual violence" and using prayer as a means of attack is that we may become the very thing we are fighting against! Tom White, an experienced counselor and speaker in spiritual warfare, observes:

> The primary activity envisioned in strategic warfare is *intercession* before the throne of God, not *interaction* with fallen principalities. We *are not* called to wield laser beams of biblical authority to destroy heavenly strongholds. We *are* called to destroy in the lives of people (Christian and non-Christian) "strongholds, . . . arguments and every pretension that sets itself up against the knowledge of God" (2 Cor. 10:4-5). We are called to faithfully reflect the glory of Jesus Christ through our obedience to his commands.[6]

Thus, while I acknowledge the reality of hierarchies of spirits, and I delight in seeing our need to repent of those strongholds that enslave us, I do not see the justification scripturally or historically for confronting these spirits directly by discerning their names and attacking them in prayer.

The Christian's Authority on Each Front

Let's think through how our authority in Christ can be lived out on the various levels of spiritual warfare that we have explored. On the personal front, as one of God's children, I can speak with my Father's authority to the one who wants to intimidate me. In this I am not *praying* to Satan but *announcing* or *reminding* him of his place and my determination not to let him control me. I am to speak the truth of the Bible guided by the Spirit in wielding Christ's authority. I encourage you to ask God to uncover strongholds that may be in your life. When he does, go to the Scriptures to learn the truth you need to know and exercise the authority he has made available to you to break them down.

On the interpersonal front, we are entitled to employ Christ's authority over the harassed and helpless people God brings our way. However, God will not let this devolve into raw displays of power. He is concerned that, through Christ's enabling authority and power, people are empowered to fight their own battles. In that way, together we can face the enemy, secure in Christ's victory. Helping others when they are down and letting them help me when I am down keeps us working together against the common enemy we face. Do you have someone you can turn to who is willing to grow together with you in exercising God's authority against the enemy?

On the local church front, church leaders exercise God's rule over the enemy's attacks. They prepare the church for spiritual growth by grounding the people in truth and being models of delighting in God, loving others, and putting on their spiritual armor. They also watch for and expose Satan's schemes against the church and, when appropriate, stand against his work on behalf of the people.

On the systemic front, we are to walk cautiously in claiming to take authority against territorial spirits. The strength of Satan's hold on a culture or community is dependent on the extent to which the people of the community give him control over their lives by blindly accepting his strongholds over them. A church that naively tries to confront territorial spirits without breaking the back of sin in the community will get little more than an exercise in frustration. When a community is broken before God, however, the local churches will have the joy of plundering the captives of Satan in leading people to Christ. Rather than praying against spirits, then, it is better to pray for God's Spirit to break the rebellious will in human hearts and bring people to repentance before him.

You Have What It Takes to Stand Firm!

Spiritual warfare is not a one-time ritual. It is not simply a set of techniques that we call up on command. It is not a magic exercise that instantly matures us. Spiritual warfare is a lifetime battle to grow to be more like Christ and to watch him work through us to set others free so that they too might grow. It is my deepest hope that this book has enabled and equipped you with the essentials you need for that journey.

As a follower of Christ, you have all that is necessary to succeed in spiritual conflict. The truth you possess teaches you how to live and how to understand your struggles. It does not promise pat or easy answers but gives hope in the victory that God will give. If we do not act on the truth, however, it will be nothing more than head knowledge, which helps us understand things but won't empower us to defeat Satan's schemes.

My hope is that you have found new ways of thinking about God and his work in your life, the lives of your friends, your church, your community, and your culture. I hope you have also discovered new ways to think about Satan and his work in our lives and world. May these new understandings drive you back to the Bible, our only true and authoritative source book on spiritual warfare. As you walk the Christian pilgrimage, I urge you to use these essential tools of warfare to come against the enemy. Above all, use them in order to grow in your faith and to help others grow in their faith, so that together we will be better prepared for heaven.

Appendix A
Bible Verses to Memorize

The following verses have been chosen with spiritual warfare issues in mind. They focus on the truths about God, Satan, and people. If you choose to memorize some or all of them, you may want to transfer them to index cards for ready reference during the day, until they are firmly embedded in your heart. You may also want to meditate on them, giving the truth the chance to sink in deeply and take root in your heart.

Who Is God?

God is the Creator.

Nehemiah 9:6: You alone are the LORD. You made the heavens, even the highest heavens, and all their starry host, the earth and all that is on it, the seas and all that is in them. You give life to everything, and the multitudes of heaven worship you.

Psalm 24:1: The earth is the LORD's, and everything in it, the world, and all who live in it.

Colossians. 1:17: He is before all things, and in him all things hold together.

God is sovereignly in control of all the universe.

Psalm 89:5: The heavens praise your wonders, O LORD, your faithfulness too, in the assembly of the holy ones.

Psalm 103:19: The LORD has established his throne in heaven, and his kingdom rules over all.

Psalm 115:3: Our God is in heaven; he does whatever pleases him.

God's sovereignty extends to my daily life.
Psalm 139:16b: All the days ordained for me were written in your book before one of them came to be.

Proverbs 16:33: The lot is cast into the lap, but its every decision is from the LORD.

Nothing is too difficult for God.
Matthew 19:26: Jesus looked at them and said, "With man this is impossible, but with God all things are possible."

1 Corinthians 1:25: For the foolishness of God is wiser than man's wisdom, and the weakness of God is stronger than man's strength.

Jeremiah 32:27: I am the LORD, the God of all mankind. Is anything too hard for me?

God will meet my every need.
Matthew 6:30: If that is how God clothes the grass of the field, which is here today and tomorrow is thrown into the fire, will he not much more clothe you, O you of little faith?

He is my father or daddy.
Matthew 6:9: For you did not receive a spirit that makes you a slave again to fear, but you received the Spirit of sonship. And by him we cry, "Abba, Father."

He is the giver of good gifts.

Matthew 7:11: If you, then, though you are evil, know how to give good gifts to your children, how much more will your Father in heaven give good gifts to those who ask him!

James 1:17: Every good and perfect gift is from above, coming down from the Father of the heavenly lights, who does not change like shifting shadows.

He is the God of compassion and comfort.

2 Corinthians 1:3: Praise be to the God and Father of our Lord Jesus Christ, the Father of compassion and the God of all comfort.

He is patient.

2 Peter 3:9: The Lord is not slow in keeping his promise, as some understand slowness. He is patient with you, not wanting anyone to perish, but everyone to come to repentance.

He is faithful.

1 John 1:9: If we confess our sins, he is faithful and just and will forgive us our sins and purify us from all unrighteousness.

He is loving.

John 3:16: For God so loved the world that he gave his one and only Son, that whoever believes in him shall not perish but have eternal life.

He is the immortal, invisible King.

1 Timothy 1:17: Now to the King eternal, immortal, invisible, the only God, be honor and glory for ever and ever. Amen.

1 Timothy 6:15b-16: God, the blessed and only Ruler, the King of kings and Lord of lords, who alone is immortal and who lives in unapproachable light, whom no-one has seen or can see. To him be honor and might for ever. Amen.

He gives wisdom.

James 1:5: If any of you lacks wisdom, he should ask God, who gives generously to all without finding fault, and it will be given to him.

He is a God of peace.

Romans 15:13: May the God of hope fill you will all hope and peace as you trust in him.

1 Corinthians 14:33a: For God is not a God of disorder but of peace.

Who Am I?

I am God's child.

John 1:12: Yet to all who received him, to those who believed in his name, he gave the right to become children of God.

Romans 8:16: The Spirit himself testifies with our spirit that we are God's children.

I am created in God's image.

Genesis 1:27: So God created man in his own image, in the image of God he created him; male and female he created them.

I glorify him by worship.

Psalm 29:2: Ascribe to the LORD the glory due to his name; worship the LORD in the splendor of his holiness.

God has effected my rescue from Satan.

Colossians 1:13: For he has rescued us from the dominion of darkness and brought us into the kingdom of the Son he loves.

Belief in Jesus brings new life.

John 5:24: I tell you the truth, whoever hears my word and believes him who sent me has eternal life and will not be condemned; he has crossed over from death to life.

2 Corinthians 5:17: Therefore, if anyone is in Christ, he is a new creation; the old has gone, the new has come!

I am a joint heir with Christ.

Romans 8:16: Now if we are children, then we are heirs—heirs of God and co-heirs with Christ, if indeed we share in his sufferings in order that we may also share in his glory.

I am blessed by God.

Ephesians 1:3: Praise be to the God and Father of our Lord Jesus Christ, who has blessed us in the heavenly realms with every spiritual blessing in Christ.

He sealed me with his Spirit.

2 Corinthians 1:21-22: Now it is God who makes both us and you stand firm in Christ. He anointed us, set his seal of ownership on us, and put his Spirit in our hearts as a deposit, guaranteeing what is to come.

God moderates every temptation I experience.

1 Corinthians 10:13: No temptation has seized you except what is common to man. And God is faithful; he will not let you be tempted beyond what you can bear. But when you are tempted, he will also provide a way out so that you can stand up under it.

God works in me.

Romans 8:28-29: And we know that in all things God works for the good of those who love him, who have been called according to his purpose. For those God foreknew he also predestined to be conformed to the likeness of his Son, that he might be the firstborn among many brothers.

Philippians 2:13: For it is God who works in you to will and to act according to his good purpose.

He has prepared good works for me to do.

Ephesians 2:8-10: For we are God's workmanship, created in Christ Jesus to do good works, which God prepared in advance for us to do.

He is able to keep me from falling.

Jude 24: To him who is able to keep you from falling and to present you before his glorious presence without fault and with great joy.

Even when I do fall, God comforts me in my troubles.

2 Corinthians 1:3: Praise be to the God and Father of our Lord Jesus Christ, the Father of compassion and the God of all comfort, who comforts us in all our troubles.

I am seated with Christ and share his authority.

Ephesians 2:6: And God raised us up with Christ and seated us with him in the heavenly realms in Christ Jesus.

I have God's grace.

Ephesians 4:7: But to each one of us grace has been given as Christ apportioned it.

Waging Spiritual Warfare

I am to live in submission to God and resist Satan.

James 4:7: Submit yourselves, then, to God. Resist the devil, and he will flee from you.

1 Peter 5:9: Resist him, standing firm in the faith, because you know that your brothers throughout the world are undergoing the same kind of sufferings.

I am to fight Satan in God's armor.

Ephesians 6:11: Put on the full armor of God so that you can take your stand against the devil's schemes.

I am to be aware of Satan's schemes.

2 Corinthians 2:11: I have forgiven . . . in order that Satan might not outwit us. For we are not unaware of his schemes.

I am to make my thoughts captive to Christ.

2 Corinthians 10:3-5: We demolish arguments and every pretension that sets itself up against the knowledge of God, and we take captive every thought to make it obedient to Christ.

I am to overcome evil with good.

Romans 12:21: Do not be overcome by evil, but overcome evil with good.

I am to return curses with blessings.

1 Peter 3:8-9: Do not repay evil with evil or insult with insult, but with blessing, because to this you were called so that you may inherit a blessing.

I am to gently instruct those who oppose God's ways.

2 Timothy 2:24-25: And the Lord's servant must not quarrel; instead, he must be kind to everyone, able to teach, not resentful. Those who oppose him he must gently instruct, in the hope that God will grant them repentance leading them to a knowledge of the truth.

Who Is Satan?

Satan is the deceiver.

Revelation 12:9: The great dragon was hurled down—that ancient serpent called the devil, or Satan, who leads the whole world astray. He was hurled to the earth, and his angels with him.

He is an inciter.

1 Chronicles 21:1: Satan rose up against Israel and incited David to take a census of Israel.

He is an accuser.

Zechariah 3:1: Then he showed me Joshua the high priest standing before the angel of the LORD, and Satan standing at his right side to accuse him.

Revelation 12:10b: For the accuser of our brothers, who accuses them before our God day and night, has been hurled down.

He is an opportunist.

Luke 4:13: When the devil had finished all this tempting, he left him until an opportune time.

He operates only on the leash that God holds.

Job 1:12: The LORD said to Satan, "Very well, then, everything he has is in your hands, but on the man himself do not lay a finger." Then Satan went out from the presence of the LORD.

Job 2:6: The LORD said to Satan, "Very well, then, he is in your hands; but you must spare his life."

He is a sinner whose work Jesus came to destroy.

1 John 3:8a: He who does what is sinful is of the devil, because the devil has been sinning from the beginning. The reason the Son of God appeared was to destroy the devil's work.

He is a murderer and a liar.

John 8:44: You belong to your father, the devil, and you want to carry out your father's desire. He was a murderer from the beginning, not holding to the truth, for there is no truth in him. When he lies, he speaks his native language, for he is a liar and the father of lies.

He disguises himself.

2 Corinthians 11:14: And no wonder, for Satan himself masquerades as an angel of light.

He performs counterfeit signs and miracles.

2 Thessalonians 2:9: The coming of the lawless one will be in accordance with the work of Satan displayed in all kinds of counterfeit miracles, signs and wonders.

He roams the earth.

Job 1:7: The LORD said to Satan, "Where have you come from?" Satan answered the LORD, "From roaming through the earth and going to and fro in it."

He seeks prey to devour.

1 Peter 5:8: Be self-controlled and alert. Your enemy the devil prowls around like a roaring lion looking for someone to devour.

He wages war against Christians.

Revelation 12:17: Then the dragon was enraged at the woman and went off to make war against the rest of her offspring—those who obey God's commandments and hold to the testimony of Jesus.

The fear he held over us was rendered powerless by Christ.

Hebrews 2:14: Since the children have flesh and blood, he too shared in their humanity so that by his death he might destroy him who holds the power of death—that is, the devil.

Nothing will prevent his final defeat.

Matthew 25:41: Then he will say to those on his left, "Depart from me, you who are cursed, into the eternal fire prepared for the devil and his angels."

Romans 16:20: The God of peace will soon crush Satan under your feet. The grace of our Lord Jesus be with you. *Revelation. 20:10:* And the devil, who deceived them, was thrown into the lake of burning sulphur, where the beast and the false prophet had been thrown. They will be tormented day and night for ever and ever.

Appendix B
Bible Passages of People Dealing with Demons

This list is not intended to be comprehensive, but representative of the types of encounters people had with demons in the New Testament. Additionally, the passages are not given with the surrounding context, only the verses that describe the actual work being done. Key words are italicized. Several passages appear under more than one category, as they show more than one idea.

Jesus Healing the Demonized

Matthew 4:24: News about him spread all over Syria, and people brought to him all who were ill with various diseases, those suffering severe pain, the demon-possessed, those having seizures, and the paralyzed, and he *healed* them.

Matthew 15:28: Then Jesus answered, "Woman, you have great faith! Your request is granted." And her daughter was *healed* from that very hour.

Matthew 17:18: Jesus rebuked the demon, and it came out of the boy, and *he was healed* from that moment.

Luke 6:18-19: Those troubled by evil spirits were *cured*, and the people all tried to touch him, because power was coming from him and *healing* them all.

Luke 7:21: At that very time Jesus *cured* many who had diseases, sicknesses and evil spirits, and gave sight to many who were blind.

Luke 8:2: And also some women who had been *cured* of evil spirits and diseases: Mary (called Magdalene) *from whom seven demons had come out.*

Luke 8:36: Those who had seen it told the people how the demon-possessed man had been *cured.*

Luke 13:16: Then should not this woman, a daughter of Abraham, whom Satan has kept bound for eighteen long years, *be set free* on the Sabbath day from what bound her?

Jesus' Authority over Demons

Matthew 8:16: When evening came, many who were demon-possessed were brought to him, and *he drove out the spirits with a word* and healed all the sick.

Matthew 17:18: Jesus *rebuked the demon*, and it came out of the boy, and *he was healed from that moment.*

Mark 1:25, 27: *"Be quiet!"* said Jesus sternly. *"Come out of him!"* The people were all so amazed that they asked each other, "What is this? A new teaching and with authority! He even *gives orders to evil spirits and they obey him."*

Mark 1:34: And Jesus healed many who had various diseases.

He also *drove out many demons,* but *he would not let the demons speak because they knew who he was.*

Mark 5:13: He gave them permission, and the evil spirits came out and went into the pigs. The herd, about two thousand in number, rushed down the steep bank into the lake and were drowned.

Mark 9:25: When Jesus saw that a crowd was running to the scene, he *rebuked* the evil spirit. "You deaf and mute spirit," he said, *"I command you, come out of him and never enter him again."*

Luke 4:36: All the people were amazed and said to each other, "What is this teaching? *With authority and power he gives orders to evil spirits and they come out!"*

Luke 4:41: Moreover, demons came out of many people, shouting, "You are the Son of God!" But *he rebuked them and would not allow them to speak,* because they knew he was the Christ.

Jesus Driving Out Demons

Matthew 12:28: "But if *I drive out demons by the Spirit of God,* then the kingdom of God has come upon you."

Mark 5:8-9: For Jesus *had said to him, "Come out of this man, you evil spirit!"* Then Jesus *asked him, "What is your name?"* "My name is Legion," he replied, "for we are many."

Mark 9:25: When Jesus saw that a crowd was running to the scene, *he rebuked the evil spirit.* "You deaf and mute spirit," he said, *"I command you, come out of him and never enter him again."*

Luke 4:36: All the people were amazed and said to each other, "What is this teaching? *With authority and power he gives orders to evil spirits and they come out!"*

Luke 8:29: For Jesus *had commanded the evil spirit to come out of the man.*

The Apostles' Dealing with Demons

Matthew 10:1, 8: He called his twelve disciples to him and *gave them authority to drive out evil spirits and to heal every disease and sickness. . . . "Heal the sick, raise the dead, cleanse those who have leprosy, drive out demons. Freely you have received, freely give."*

Matthew 17:16: I brought him to your disciples, but *they could not heal him.*

Mark 6:13: They *drove out many demons* and *anointed many sick people with oil and healed them.*

Luke 10:17: The seventy-two returned with joy and said, "Lord, *even the demons submit to us in your name."*

Acts 5:16: Crowds gathered also from the towns around Jerusalem, bringing their sick and *those tormented by evil spirits, and all of them were healed.*

Paul

Acts 16:18: She kept this up for many days. Finally Paul became so troubled that he turned round and said to the spirit, *"In the name of Jesus Christ I command you to come out of her!"* At that moment the spirit left her.

Acts 19:11-12: God did extraordinary miracles through Paul, so that *even handkerchiefs and aprons that had touched him were taken to the sick, and their illnesses were cured and the evil spirits left them.*

Anonymous Man

Luke 9:49: "Master," said John, "we saw a man driving out demons *in your name and we tried to stop him, because he is not one of us."*

Philip

Acts 8:7: With shrieks, evil spirits came out of many, and many paralytics and cripples were healed.

False Christians

Matthew 7:22: Many will say to me on that day, "Lord, Lord, did we not prophesy in your name, and *in your name drive out demons and perform many miracles?"*

All Christians

2 Corinthians 10:4-5: The weapons we fight with are not the weapons of the world. On the contrary, they have divine power to demolish strongholds. We demolish arguments and every pretension that sets itself up against the knowledge of God, and *we take captive every thought to make it obedient to Christ.*

Ephesians 6:13-18: Therefore *put on the full armor of God,* so that when the day of evil comes, you may be able to stand your ground, and after you have done everything, to stand.

Stand firm then, with the belt of *truth* buckled round your waist, with the breastplate of *righteousness* in place, and with your feet fitted with the readiness that comes from the *gospel of peace*. In addition to all this, take up the shield of *faith*, with which you can extinguish all the flaming arrows of the evil one. Take the helmet of *salvation* and the *sword of the Spirit, which is the word of God.* And *pray in the Spirit on all occasions with all kinds of prayers and requests. With this in mind, be alert and always keep on praying for all the saints.*

James 4:7: Submit yourselves, then, to God. *Resist the devil,* and he will flee from you.

1 Peter 5:8-9: Be self-controlled and alert. Your enemy the devil prowls around like a roaring lion looking for someone to devour. *Resist him, standing firm in the faith,* because you know that your brothers throughout the world are undergoing the same kind of sufferings.

Revelation 12:10b-11: For the accuser of our brothers, who accuses them before our God day and night, has been hurled down. They overcame him *by the blood of the Lamb and by the word of their testimony; they did not love their lives so much as to shrink from death.*

Appendix C

Bible Passages of Demonic Activity in People

This list is categorized by the strategies and actions used by the enemy. It is not intended to be comprehensive, but representative of the types of encounters people had with demons in the New Testament. Additionally, passages are not given with the surrounding context, only the verses that describe the actual work being done. Key words are italicized. Some passages appear under more than one category, as they show more than one idea.

Tempt, Deceive, Outwit

2 Corinthians 2:10b-11: And what I have forgiven—if there was anything to forgive—I have forgiven in the sight of Christ for your sake, in order that *Satan might not outwit us*. For we are not unaware of his schemes.

1 Thessalonians 3:5: I was afraid that in some way *the tempter might have tempted you* and our efforts might have been useless.

1 Timothy 2:14: And Adam was not the one deceived; it was the woman *who was deceived* and became a sinner.

Attack

Luke 22:31: Jesus said, "Simon, Simon, Satan has asked *to sift you* as wheat."

2 Corinthians 12:7: To keep me from becoming conceited because of these surpassingly great revelations, there was given me *a thorn in my flesh, a messenger of Satan, to torment me.*

1 Thessalonians 2:18 (NRSV): For we wanted to come to you—certainly I, Paul, wanted to again and again—*but Satan blocked our way.*

1 Peter 5:8: Be self-controlled and alert. Your enemy the devil prowls around like a roaring lion looking for someone *to devour.*

Enslave

Acts 5:3: Then Peter said, "Ananias, how is it that *Satan has so filled your heart* that you have lied to the Holy Spirit and have kept for yourself some of the money you received for the land?"

Galatians 4:9 (NRSV): How can you turn back again to the weak and beggarly elemental spirits? How can you want to *be enslaved to them* again?

Colossians 2:8 (NRSV): See to it that *no one takes you captive* through philosophy and empty deceit, according to human tradition, according to the elemental spirits of the universe, and not according to Christ.

Blind, Lead Astray

Acts 10:38: . . . and how [Jesus] went around doing good and healing all who were *under the power of the devil,* because God was with him.

1 Corinthians 12:2 (NRSV): You know that when you were pagans, *you were enticed and led astray* to idols that could not speak.

2 Corinthians 4:4: The *god of this age has blinded the minds of unbelievers,* so that they cannot see the light of the gospel of the glory of Christ, who is the image of God.

Ephesians 2:2: . . . in which you used to live when you followed the ways of this world and of the ruler of the kingdom of the air, the spirit *who is now at work in those who are disobedient.*

2 Timothy 2:26: . . . and that they will come to their senses and escape from the trap of the devil, *who has taken them captive to do his will.*

Revelation 12:9: The great dragon was hurled down—that ancient serpent called the devil, or Satan, who *leads the whole world astray.*

Torture, Afflict, Torment, Blind

Matthew 12:22 (NRSV): Then they brought to him *a demoniac who was blind and mute*; and he cured him, so that the one who had been mute could speak and see.

Matthew 15:22 (NRSV): Just then a Canaanite woman from that region came out and started shouting, "Have mercy on me, Lord, Son of David; my daughter *is tormented by a demon."*

Mark 9:17-18: A man in the crowd answered, "Teacher, I brought you my son, who is possessed by *a spirit that has robbed him of speech.* Whenever *it seizes him, it throws him to the ground.* He foams at the mouth, gnashes his teeth and becomes rigid. I asked your disciples to drive out the spirit, but they could not."

Luke 6:18: Those *troubled by evil spirits* were cured.

Luke 8:29: (For many times *it had seized him;* he was kept under guard and bound with chains and shackles, but he would break the bonds and *be driven by the demon into the wilds.*)

Luke 9:42: Even while the boy was coming, *the demon threw him to the ground in a convulsion.* But Jesus rebuked the evil spirit, healed the boy and gave him back to his father.

Luke 13:16: "Then should not this woman, a daughter of Abraham, whom *Satan has kept bound* for eighteen long years, be set free on the Sabbath day from what bound her?"

Acts 5:16: Crowds gathered also from the towns around Jerusalem, bringing their sick and *those tormented by evil spirits,* and all of them were healed.

Endnotes

Chapter 5: Facing the Enemy

1. Heinrich Schlier, *Principalities and Powers in the New Testament* (New York: Herder and Herder, 1961), p. 58.

2. Nigel Wright, *The Satan Syndrome: Putting the Power of Darkness in Its Place* (Grand Rapids: Zondervan, 1990), p. 25.

3. Otto Weber, *Foundations of Dogmatics,* vol. 1, trans. Darryl L. Guder (Grand Rapids: Eerdmans, 1981), p. 489.

4. George Barna, *What Americans Believe: An Annual Survey of Values and Religious Views in the United States* (Ventura, Calif.: Regal Books, 1991), pp. 204–206.

Chapter 6: Who Are the Targets?

1. The entire story is told in Steve Sjogren's *Conspiracy of Kindness* (Ann Arbor, Mich.: Vine Books, 1993). Sjogren addresses this approach to spiritual warfare further in *Servant Warfare* (Ann Arbor, Mich.: Vine Books, 1996).

Chapter 7: Unmasking Our Sin

1. Dan Allender and Tremper Longman, *Bold Love* (Colorado Springs, Colo.: NavPress, 1992), p. 53.

2. C. S. Lewis, *Mere Christianity* (New York: Macmillan, 1952), pp. 108–109.

3. John White, *Changing on the Inside* (Ann Arbor, Mich.: Servant, 1991), p. 77.

Chaper 8: Putting Sin Behind Us

1. C. S. Lewis, *The Screwtape Letters* (New York: Macmillan, 1961), p. 56.

Chapter 9: Loving and Enjoying God

1. Tim Hansel, *You Gotta Keep Dancing* (Elgin, Ill.: Chariot, 1985), p. 41.
2. John White, *Changing on the Inside* (Ann Arbor, Mich.: Servant, 1991), pp. 137–38.

Chapter 10: Loving and Enjoying People

1. For some of these ideas I am indebted to Carol Schultz, whose paper on personal forgiveness clarified several issues for me.
2. The main ideas for these questions came from Charles Stanley's sermon series "How to Experience Forgiveness" (Atlanta: In Touch Ministries, 1988).
3. Statement taken from Neil Anderson's *The Steps to Freedom in Christ* (Ventura, Calif.: Gospel Light, 1996), p. 2.
4. These steps are adapted from David A. Stoop and James Masteller's book *Forgiving Our Parents, Forgiving Ourselves: Healing Adult Children of Dysfunctional Families* (Ann Arbor, Mich.: Vine Books, 1991).
5. This story is a summary account taken from a paper by John Watson. See Charles Kraft and Mark White's book, *Behind Enemy Lines* (Ann Arbor, Mich.: Servant, 1994), for the full version.

Chapter 11: Putting on God's Armor

1. David M. Lloyd-Jones, *The Christian Soldier: An Exposition of Ephesians 6:10-20* (Edinburgh: The Banner of Truth Trust, 1977), p. 305.

Chapter 12: The Christian's Authority

1. Walter Wink, *Engaging the Powers: Discernment and Resistance in a World of Domination* (Minneapolis, Minn.: Fortress Press, 1996), chap. 1.

2. My ideas on this topic were enhanced by a paper on spiritual binding by Jim Apker.

Chapter 13: Fighting the Good Fight

1. Oswald Sanders, *Satan Is No Myth* (Chicago: Moody Press, 1983).

2. Neil Anderson and Charles Mylander, *Setting Your Church Free: A Biblical Plan to Help Your Church* (Ventura, Calif.: Regal Books, 1994), p. 128.

3. C. Peter Wagner, *Confronting the Powers* (Ventura, Calif.: Regal Books, 1996), p. 46.

4. The best discussion on the topic of territorial spirits I have seen to date is found in Clinton Arnold's book *Three Crucial Questions about Spiritual Warfare* (Grand Rapids: Baker Book House, 1997).

5. The term "spiritual mapping" was popularized by George Otis. See "An Overview of Spiritual Mapping" in *Breaking Strongholds in Your City* (Ventura, Calif.: Regal Books, 1993), pp. 29–48.

6. Tom White, *Breaking Strongholds: How Spiritual Warfare Sets Captives Free* (Ann Arbor, Mich.: Vine Books, 1993), pp. 141–42.

Bibliography

Allender, Dan, and Tremper Longman. *Bold Love.* Colorado Springs, Colo.: NavPress, 1992.

Anderson, Neil. *The Bondage Breaker.* Eugene, Ore.: Harvest House, 1990.

_____. *Living Free in Christ.* Ventura, Calif.: Gospel Light, 1993.

_____. *Resolving Personal Conflicts.* LaHabra, Calif.: Freedom in Christ Ministries, n.d.

_____. *The Steps to Freedom in Christ.* Ventura, Calif.: Gospel Light, 1996.

_____. *Victory over the Darkness: Realizing the Power of Your Identity in Christ.* Ventura, Calif.: Regal Books, 1990.

_____. *Walking Through the Darkness.* San Bernardino, Calif.: Here's Life Publishers, 1991.

Anderson, Neil, and Charles Mylander. *Setting Your Church Free: A Biblical Plan to Help Your Church.* Ventura, Calif.: Regal Books, 1994.

Arnold, Clinton E. *Ephesians: Power and Magic, The Concept of Power in Ephesians in Light of Its Historical Setting.* Grand Rapids: Baker Book House, 1992.

_____. *Powers of Darkness: Principalities and Powers in Paul's Letters.* Downers Grove, Ill.: InterVarsity Press, 1992.

_____. *Three Crucial Questions about Spiritual Warfare.* Grand Rapids: Baker Book House, 1997.

Barna, George. *What Americans Believe: An Annual Survey of Values and Religious Views in the United States.* Ventura, Calif.: Regal Books, 1991.

Bellah, Robert N. *Habits of the Heart: Individualism and Commitment in American Life.* San Francisco: Harper & Row, 1985.

Bubeck, Mark I. *The Adversary.* Chicago: Moody Press, 1975.

_____. *Overcoming the Adversary.* Chicago: Moody Press, 1984.

_____. *The Satanic Revival.* San Bernardino, Calif.: Here's Life
Publishers, 1991.

Carter, Stephen L. *The Culture of Disbelief: How American Law
and Politics Trivialize Religious Devotion.* New York: Basic
Books, 1993.

Cloud, Henry, and John Townsend. *Boundaries: When to Say
YES, When to Say NO to Take Control of Your Life.* Grand
Rapids: Zondervan, 1992.

Guinness, Os. *The American Hour: A Time of Reckoning and the
Once and Future Role of Faith.* New York: The Free Press,
1993.

Hansel, Tim. *You Gotta Keep on Dancing.* Elgin, Ill.: David C.
Cook, 1985.

Hiebert, Paul. *Anthropological Reflections on Missiological Issues.* Grand Rapids: Baker Book House, 1994.

Hofstede, Geert. *Cultures and Organizations: Software of the
Mind.* New York: McGraw-Hill Book Company, 1991.

Keyes, Richard. "The Idol Factory." In *No God but God: Breaking with the Idols of Our Age.* Edited by Os Guinness and John
Seel. Chicago: Moody Press, 1992.

Korem, Danny, and Paul Meier. *The Fakers: Exploding the
Myths of the Supernatural.* Grand Rapids: Baker Book House,
1980.

Kraft, Charles H. *Christianity with Power: Your Worldview and
Your Experience of the Supernatural.* Ann Arbor, Mich.: Vine
Books, 1989.

_____. *Defeating Dark Angels: Breaking Demonic Oppression
in the Believer's Life.* Ann Arbor, Mich.: Vine Books, 1992.

Lewis, C. S. *Mere Christianity.* New York: Macmillan Publishing Company, 1952.

_____. *The Screwtape Letters.* New York: Macmillan Publishing
Company, 1961.

Lloyd-Jones, David M. *The Christian Soldier: An Exposition of Ephesians 6:10-20*. Edinburgh: The Banner of Truth Trust, 1977.

Logan, Jim. *Reclaiming Surrendered Ground: Protecting Your Family from Spiritual Attacks*. Chicago: Moody Press, 1995.

MacArthur, John. *How to Meet the Enemy: Arming Yourself for Spiritual Warfare*. Wheaton, Ill.: Victor Books, 1992.

Moreau, A. Scott. "Evil Spirits: Biblical and Practical Issues." *Urban Mission*, December 1995, pp. 25–36.

_____. *The World of the Spirits*. Nairobi, Kenya: Evangel Publishing House, 1990.

Needham, David C. *Birthright: Christian Do You Know Who You Are?* Portland, Ore.: Multnomah Press, 1979.

Page, Sydney H. T. *Powers of Evil: A Biblical Study of Satan and Demons*. Grand Rapids: Baker Book House, 1995.

Piper, John. *Desiring God: Meditations of a Christian Hedonist*. Portland, Ore.: Multnomah Press, 1986.

_____. *Let the Nations Be Glad! The Supremacy of God in Missions*. Grand Rapids: Baker Book House, 1993.

Powilson, David. *Power Encounters: Reclaiming Spiritual Warfare*. Grand Rapids: Baker Book House, 1995.

Schlier, Heinrich, *Principalities and Powers in the New Testament*. New York: Herder and Herder, 1961.

Sjogren, Steve. *Conspiracy of Kindness*. Ann Arbor, Mich.: Vine Books, 1993.

_____. *Servant Warfare*. Ann Arbor, Mich.: Vine Books, 1996.

Stoop, David A., and James Masteller. *Forgiving Our Parents, Forgiving Ourselves: Healing Adult Children of Dysfunctional Families*. Ann Arbor, Mich.: Vine Books, 1991.

Wagner, C. Peter, ed. *Breaking Strongholds in Your City*. Ventura, Calif.: Regal Books, 1993.

_____. *Confronting the Powers*. Ventura, Calif.: Regal Books, 1996.

_____, ed. *Engaging the Enemy: How to Fight and Defeat Territorial Spirits*. Ventura, Calif.: Regal Books, 1991.

_____. *Warfare Prayer: How to Seek God's Power and Protection in the Battle to Build His Kingdom*. Ventura, Calif.: Regal Books, 1992.

Warner, Timothy. *Spiritual Warfare: Victory over the Powers of This Dark World*. Wheaton, Ill.: Crossway Books, 1991.

White, John. *Changing on the Inside*. Ann Arbor, Mich.: Servant Publications, 1991.

_____. *The Fight: A Practical Handbook for Christian Living*. Downers Grove, Ill.: InterVarsity Press, 1976.

White, Tom. *Breaking Strongholds: How Spiritual Warfare Sets Captives Free*. Ann Arbor, Mich.: Vine Books, 1993.

Whitney, Donald S. *Spiritual Disciplines for the Christian Life*. Colorado Springs, Colo.: NavPress, 1991.

Wink, Walter. *Engaging the Powers: Discernment and Resistance in a World of Domination*. Minneapolis, Minn.: Fortress Press, 1992

Wright, Nigel. *The Satan Syndrome: Putting the Power of Darkness in Its Place*. Grand Rapids: Zondervan, 1990.

Index